MAY

TWILIGHT IN THE KINGDOM

TWILIGHT IN THE KINGDOM

UNDERSTANDING THE SAUDIS

Mark A. Caudill
Foreword by Steve Coll

PRAEGER SECURITY INTERNATIONAL
Westport, Connecticut • London

Library of Congress Cataloging-in-Publication Data

Caudill, Mark A., 1963–
  Twilight in the kingdom: understanding the Saudis /
Mark A. Caudill; foreword by Steve Coll.
      p. cm.
  Includes bibliographical references and index.
  ISBN 0-275-99252-7 (alk. paper)
  1. Saudi Arabia—Civilization. 2. Saudi Arabia—Social
life and customs. I. Title.
  DS215.c35 2006
  953.8—dc22   2006015107

British Library Cataloguing in Publication Data is available.

Library of Congress Catalog Card Number: 2006015107
ISBN: 0-275-99252-7

First published in 2006.

Praeger Security International, 88 Post Road West, Westport, CT 06881
An imprint of Greenwood Publishing Group, Inc.
www.praeger.com

Printed in the United States of America

The paper used in this book complies with the
Permanent Paper Standard issued by the National
Information Standards Organization (Z39.48–1984).

10 9 8 7 6 5 4 3 2 1

For my father
and for the Foreign Service National employees
of the U.S. Consulate General in Jeddah, Saudi Arabia,
who were killed and wounded in an attack by terrorists
on December 6, 2004

Contents

Foreword *by Steve Coll*   *ix*

Acknowledgments   *xi*

Map of Saudi Arabia   *xii*

Introduction: Bricks and Mortar   *xiii*

Chapter 1. Life and Death   *1*
    Marriage, Money, and Men of Modest Means   *3*
    Flowers for Ousman   *7*
    The Life of Spice   *10*

Chapter 2. Holy Cities   *17*
    Medina Yesterday and Today   *21*
    The Kiswa   *27*
    The King's Highway   *31*
    The Darb Zubaydah   *37*
    The Mawaqeet   *41*

Chapter 3. The Hajj   *47*
    Soup to Nuts   *51*
    Mecca Prepares for Pilgrims   *59*
    A Pilgrim's Journal   *63*

Chapter 4. God and Man   *73*
        Magic   *75*
        Lawyers, Courts, and Sharia   *79*
        Debating Religious Freedom   *84*
        A Matter of Interpretation   *89*
        Whisperers   *91*
        The Hejazi Origins of Wahhabi Intolerance   *95*

Chapter 5. Hinterlands   *103*
        How Green Is My Valley   *107*
        Land of Water, Fire, and Ire   *113*
        See Rock City   *116*
        Tribalism in the Asir   *121*

Chapter 6. Rhyme and Reason   *125*
        Human Rights   *127*

Notes   *129*

Glossary   *135*

Bibliographic Note   *143*

Index   *145*

Foreword

Saudi Arabia is a young country that is exceedingly difficult for out-siders to understand. It was largely an illiterate society until half a cen-tury ago; it has no robust national history written and rewritten by its own scholars. Even innocuous books by Saudi or other Arab authors are routinely banned from distribution in the Kingdom by religious and political authorities. The normal portals through which an outsider might attempt to enter a foreign culture—a free press, independent scholarship, social or human rights activists—are faint specters, if they exist at all. Indeed, there is little tradition of public discourse of any kind in the Kingdom, other than that created and managed by the royal family, such as its recent series of National Dialogues, which so far have amounted to little more than authorized lectures to the public from the ruling Al Saud family and its allies. The government also maintains a tight grip on the press. There is no legal political opposition to the Al Saud; what little underground pamphleteering takes place mainly involves obscure debates among dissident Islamic clergy. On top of all this, Saudi society is innately reticent. Family, kin, and tribe are by far the most important sources of identity and affiliation in Arabia. There may be free and raucous debate within these groups, but it is a private discourse, carefully protected so that rivals cannot exploit it.

For all of these reasons, for the past century, the most revealing writ-ing about Saudi Arabia has often been produced by diplomats accred-ited in the Kingdom, whose freedom to travel and inquire has been tolerated, if at times reluctantly, by the Al Saud. The Dutch diplomat D. Van der Meulen's extraordinary travelogues and political reporting from the 1920s through the 1940s is perhaps the best example of the enduring value of this correspondence. Even the notorious H. St. John Philby, an erratic British courtier and businessman who lived in the Kingdom for several decades and published many books (and who was the father of the Soviet spy Kim Philby), seems essential half a century after his expulsion from the peninsula, in part because there are so few alternative sources. During the more recent period of oil booms and Saudi modernization drives, many more Westerners than in the past have lived in the Kingdom, but most of them have been businessmen or military advisers, relegated to walled compounds where they live utterly apart from Saudi Arabia, to each side's contentment. A few journalists have managed to stay long enough to slip under the Kingdom's surfaces; one of them, Peter Theroux, in *Sandstorms*, has produced one of the best pieces of observed reporting about Saudi Arabia during the last several decades. But the list of such achievements is very short.

To it now can be added Mark Caudill's *Twilight in the Kingdom*, a work of diplomatic reporting in the tradition of Van der Meulen. Caudill had studied Saudi Arabia for years before he was posted there; once in Jeddah, he lived in the city, away from the foreigners' compounds, and between his diplomatic accreditation and his natural curiosity, he was spurred to travel and explore Saudi Arabia in ways few Westerners ever do. He has produced a rare and consistently delightful tour of the Saudi Arabia that lies behind the Kingdom's clichéd façade of oil sheikhs and raging religious radicals—a troubled, and at the same time self-confident world of family, marriage, and faith, a culture the insecure Saudi government has attempted to shape and control with mixed success.

The Hejaz, which refers to the Western region of the modern Kingdom, conquered by the Al Saud in 1926, has long held itself apart from the austere central desert plateau around Riyadh where power in Saudi Arabia resides. While the Saudis and their xenophobic tribal allies fought to keep the outside world at bay, Hejazis welcomed the world to their shores, as seafaring traders and as hosts of the annual Islamic ritual, the hajj, which Caudill unforgettably describes from a participant's point of view. Although the Saudis have used their oil wealth and unchallenged political power to impose much of their severe and austere culture on the relatively eclectic and tolerant Hejaz, they have certainly not conquered the Hejazi state of mind, or the region's sense of independent identity and potential. If a day does arrive when the Al Saud lose their grip on their young Kingdom, we may yet see the Hejazi twilight of Caudill's apt formulation returned to a new dawn. In these dispatches, then, lies not only a rich sense of the present and the past, but the glimpse of a possible future, too.

Steve Coll

Acknowledgments

This book would not have been written without the support of family, friends, and colleagues. These include my mother, Ambassador Richard Baltimore, Faiza Saleh Ambah, Art Mills, John Dinkelman, Catheline Garrity, Michael Snowden, Gwen Zanin, James Blitch, Jr., Heidi Barron, Carol Dumaine, Carl Deckert, and Julie Cohen. I thank fellow Foreign Service Officer Lisa Carle for the idea and Hilary Claggett of Praeger Security International for the vote of confidence. I owe special thanks to my wife Meg and to our children, Drew and Evie, for understanding my need to understand.

I am most indebted, of course, to the many Hejazis who made it possible for me not only to learn about, but also to experience, the tremendous diversity that exists beneath the veneer of Saudi conformity in western Arabia. Their resilience never failed to impress me, and their patience remains something about which I still marvel. I hope they and all readers will forgive any errors in this work, for which I alone am responsible.

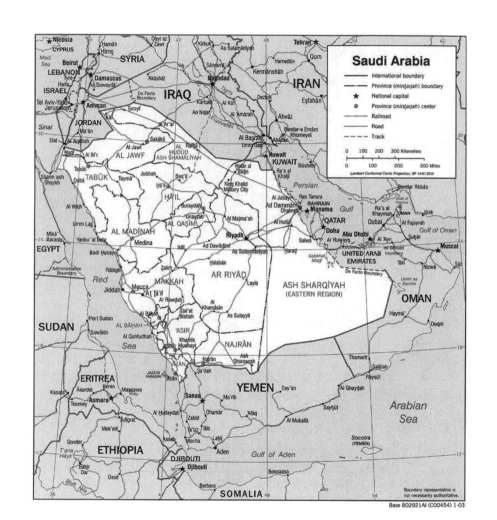

Saudi Arabia

— International boundary
—·— Province (*minṭaqah*) boundary
★ National capital
⊛ Province (*minṭaqah*) center
⊦⊦⊦⊦ Railroad
— Road
- - - Track

0   100   200   300 Kilometers
0   100   200   300 Miles
Lambert Conformal Conic Projection, SP 14N/32N

Nicosia
CYPRUS
Med. Sea   Beirut
LEBANON   Tyre
ISRAEL   Haifa   Damascus
Tel Aviv-Yafo   Amman
Jerusalem
JORDAN   Ma'ān
Sinai
Elat   Al 'Aqabah   Sakākā
Ḥa'il   Al Bi'r
Sharm ash Shaykh   Tabūk   Dubā   TABŪK
Al Wajh
Umm Laj   HĀ'IL
Minā'
Baranis   Yanbu' al Baḥr   AL MADĪNAH   Medina
EGYPT   Badr Ḥunayn
Administrative Boundary   Rābigh
Red   Mecca   MAKKAH
Jiddah   Al Tā'if   Ar Rawḍah
Port Sudan   Al Bāḥah   Al Khamāsīn
SUDAN   AL BĀḤAH
Sawākin   Al Qunfudhah   'ASIR
Khamis Mushayt
Sea   JĀZĀN
ERITREA   JAZĀ'IR FARASĀN   Jāzān
Kasala   Ākurdet   Keren   Massawa
Teseney   Asmara
Adigrat   Al Ḥudaydah   Zabid   Dhamār
Mek'elē   Ta'izz   Ibb
Gonder   Assab   Mocha   Laḥij
T'ana Hāyk'   ETHIOPIA
Baḥir Dar   Desē
Blue Nile   Berbera
SOMALIA

Ḥamāh   Ḍayr az Zawr   Kirkūk   As Sulaymānīyah   Tehran
Ḥimṣ   SYRIA   Sāmarrā   Hamedān   Qom
'Akāshāt   Baghdad   Kermānshāh   IRAN
As Suwaydā'   De Facto Boundary   IRAQ   Tigris   Dezfūl   Eṣfahān
Kāf   Ṭurayf   Karbalā   Al Kūt
An Najaf   Al 'Amārah   Ahvāz
'Ar'ar   Euphrates   Al Baṣrah   Bandar-e Emām Khomeynī
Abadan
Umm Qaṣr
Al Jawf   Al Rafhā   Kuwait   KUWAIT   Būshehr
HUDŪD ASH SHAMĀLĪYAH   Ḥafar al Bāṭin   Ra's al Khafjī
AL JAWF   Jubbah   Baq'ā'   Persian   Bandar 'Abbās
Ṭaymā'   King Khalid Military City   Al Jubayl   Ras Tanura   Strait of Hormuz
Hā'il   Buraydah   Al Majma'ah   Ad Dammām   BAHRAIN   Ra's al Khaymah   OMAN   Jāsk
'Unayzah   Al Hufūf   Dhahrān   Manama   Gulf   Dubai   Al Fujayrah
AL QAṢĪM   Riyadh   QATAR   Gulf of Oman
Doha   Abu Dhabi   Al 'Ayn   Ṣuḥār   Muscat
'Afif   Ad Dawādimī   Salwā   Ar Ruways   no defined boundary
As Sulaymānīyah   Ḥaraḍ   UNITED ARAB   'Ibrī   Nizwā   Ṣūr
Zalim   Halabān   Sabkhat Maṭṭī   EMIRATES   De Facto Boundary
AR RIYĀḌ   Layla   Umm as Samīm
ASH SHARQĪYAH   (EASTERN REGION)   OMAN
Dal'at Bishah   As Sulayyil   Haymā'   Duqm
NAJRĀN   Ash Sharawrah   Thamarit   Ṣalālah
Najrān   Raysūt
Ṣa'dah
Sanaa   Ma'rib   YEMEN   Say'ūn   Al Ghaydah   Arabian Sea
Sayḥūt
'Atāq   Al Mukallā   Socotra (YEMEN)
Aden   Gulf of Aden   Boosaaso
DJIBOUTI   Djibouti

Boundary representation is not necessarily authoritative.

Base 802921AI (C00454) 1-03

Introduction: Bricks and Mortar

I wrote this book to shed some light on what the U.S. government was learning about Saudi Arabia in the critical periods preceding and following September 11, 2001. American policymakers were, understandably, preoccupied with numerous other domestic and foreign challenges before the attacks. Afterward, although their focus quickly shifted to combating terrorism, it seemed to me that the nature of the enemy we faced and the origins of the hatred we inspired were not grasped. I believe history will show that our leaders should have paid closer attention to developments in the Hejaz, Saudi Arabia's western-most province.

Between September 1999 and July 2002, I served as an American diplomat at the U.S. Consulate General in Jeddah. This ancient Hejazi port city is the Kingdom's second largest urban area, its commercial hub, and its former capital. As a political officer, part of my job was to explain to policymakers in Washington—via classified and sometimes unclassified dispatches, of which this volume is a lightly edited compilation—the historical, religious, and political factors affecting both rulers and the ruled in western Saudi Arabia. To understand the Hejaz and convey its realities with empathy and accuracy, I felt that it was essential to go as a Muslim and participate in the spiritual lives of the locals. I made *shahadah,* the Islamic profession of faith, at a mosque in suburban Washington, DC, before departing for my post.

I roamed far and wide in the Hejaz, much of the time incognito. Fortunate to have dark hair and eyes, I grew a beard, dressed in *mufti*, and—with accented Arabic that, along with pale skin, led my contacts to believe I could be Syrian—set out to understand as much as possible about a people widely misunderstood in the West. I adopted the Saudi male custom of wearing an agate stone, set in a silver band, on the small finger of my right hand (seen as a sign of piety because it was a traditional practice, or *sunna* of the Prophet Muhammad) and become adept at judging the economic and social standing of men in the marketplace and other urban forums by the quality of their wristwatches, cufflinks, fountain pens, and *ghutras,* or Bedouin headdresses, the costliest of which featured discreet indications of their having been acquired at swank Saville Row shops or Parisian couture boutiques. In the countryside, of course, such luxuries were few and far between and, as in medieval Europe, the relative economic status of individuals more often was indicated by the quality of meat in their diets and how frequently they bathed.

I believe it is important to note upfront that the Saudis are not one people but many. Like other nations, the modern Kingdom—which in the rulers' reckoning dates from 1901, the year King Abd al-Aziz set out from exile in Kuwait to reconquer tribal lands in and around Riyadh and fulfill what members of the Al Saud family maintain is their divine mission to unite the tribes of Arabia under the aegis of ultraconservative, Wahhabi Islam—absorbed newcomers as it acquired territories and attracted visitors. Unlike most lands, however, Saudi Arabia lies in the vise-grip of an official conformity that limits what outsiders can see of its internal dynamics. Dress, religion, language, and behavior are strictly controlled and enforced through a pyramidal peer pressure, which serves constantly to reinforce the idea that all benefits and opportunities stem solely from the ruling family and its allies among the country's elite merchant clans.

I made it my mission to peel away the veneer of this conformity to expose the diversity beneath, warts and all. Its success hinged on my ability to overcome my interlocutors' fear of going too far, of revealing too much to the outsider. Becoming a Muslim and adopting, as far as possible, the daily routines and habits of the Saudis among whom I lived was, I found, the only effective way for me to overcome steep social, religious, and political barriers and get to the truth. This is not to say that there was a dearth of information about the Kingdom available to analysts. The problem, however, was that the great majority of "facts" to be had were rarely objective or reliable. Too often, I felt, the

American policymaking process relied exclusively on the self-serving utterances of Saudis educated in the West and familiar with its ways to inform their views of the Kingdom. This top-down approach (for, by and large, Saudis with degrees from prestigious American universities populate the upper reaches of society) effectively buttressed and perpetuated the Al Saud–sanctioned view of the Kingdom, its history, and its place in the world. With the wealthy and connected accounting for such a small proportion, perhaps 10 percent out of a population estimated at some 21 million, I found it incomprehensible that U.S. officials were not more willing to drill down to reach and listen to the silent majority that, as the events of September 11, 2001, demonstrated, was infused with anti-Western rage.

I determined to work in the reverse, from the bottom up. I sought to understand the Saudis where I lived, the Hejaz, as they understood themselves. This required participating intimately in my contacts' daily lives and routines. Attending prayers as often as possible at neighborhood mosques gave me exposure to previously unplumbed societal strata. Some mosques, for example, catered almost exclusively to South Asian guest workers, others to Egyptians, and still others to Yemeni and Sudanese illegal aliens. The most interesting, of course, were those tucked away in solidly middleclass and lower-middleclass Saudi neighborhoods. Not coincidentally, these also were the most closely monitored by the authorities. As the "Islamic Awakening" protests of the early 1990s showed, the Kingdom's rulers ignored (at their own peril) the discontent of citizens who did not benefit from the fabulous oil wealth that lapped the shores of Arabia in the boom years of the 1970s and early 1980s and who most keenly felt the pinch of declining oil revenues (amid official graft and exponential population growth) beginning in the mid-1980s.[1]

I liken the edifice of U.S.-Saudi relations, at the person-to-person level, to a building built of brick. Take any two individual pieces of masonry and they look alike. Pile them up and distinguishing where each was made becomes futile and pointless. But notice that, for their similarities and closeness, no two bricks touch. Each is separated from the others around it by a thin line of mortar. To a Saudi raised in the Hejaz, that mortar is a manifestation of U.S. gall and hubris. The American is a showoff; a know-it-all; a scary, rude, and profane lout who nonetheless is showered at all turns with favor by a God who must have lost his mind. The American view of Saudis is hardly more kind. The mortar represents Arabian corruption and backwardness. Even the most tolerant and worldly of my diplomatic colleagues regarded the

Saudi as an immature, lazy, benighted hypocrite who, somehow, had the good fortune to be born in a land filled with oil by a God who must have lost his mind. Of course, the mortar separates like from like as well, preventing—as any prejudice does—a complete understanding of one's self and society. But that is a topic for another time.

For now, it is enough to understand that although we and the Saudis do not touch each other, neither can we be separated without bringing the whole structure down. For better or for worse, I fear, Saudis and Americans will be stuck together for some time. I doubt we will ever be entirely comfortable with each other. We may never understand how they feel and they may never come to grips with how we think. But for partners who rely on one another for so much—we on them for oil, they on us for defense—does the absence of 100 percent clarity in our relationship with "the other" really necessitate the wrecking ball? Like most reasonable observers of the bilateral relationship, I argue that the bricks, and the mortar, should stay put. The building, a symbol of what two cultures can accomplish together despite their differences, is too important to knock down. Although perhaps less a lighthouse of understanding than a modest monument to mutual forbearance, it deserves to stand so that our heirs can see what is possible when we decide to set perfection aside and work to sustain that which is good.

Unfortunately, there will always be those for whom nothing less than the ideal is sufficient. The desire to convert the human condition into a replica of or launch pad for reaching heaven appears innate to both Americans and Saudis. From Salem to Waco, New World zealots have shown they cannot accept limits where the mind can imagine perfection. For Hejazis, the Kingdom's embrace and propagation of Wahhabism, Islam's most puritanical and uncompromising sect, is the most obvious manifestation of this same impulse. Americans have tended to see their own government or, sometimes, themselves as wanting and have acted with violence to clear the stage for God to rule directly. Hejazis have, too, and most of the terrorism modern Saudi Arabia has witnessed has come from fanatics seeking to bring on the "End of Days" and usher in a bright new world in which they, not incidentally, sit at God's right hand to judge the shortcomings of their real and imagined tormentors in this life.

Hejazi extremists differ from their American confreres in one critical respect: The compulsion to self-assess, the cultural forest in which we wander (albeit if often only rhetorically), is absent from the Saudi psychic landscape. I would like to think the fact that we look to ourselves first and tend to accept responsibility for our shortcomings is a trait inherent in a democratic society. Less charitably, maybe Freud has so pervaded our thinking that we cannot help but to peer within before lashing out. Not so the Saudis. Freed from responsibility by a paternalistic and centralized political order, absolved from blame by the resort to fatalism, my Hejazi contacts were never averse to tagging the West in general, and the United States in particular, with all manner of sinful schemes, most of which had—as their ultimate if preposterous aim—the eternal subjugation of Muslims.

Did they really believe what they said? Did they honestly think that the Pentagon spent much of its time and money looking for ways to outflank Islam? That the White House burned the midnight oil devising new and ingenious tactics for the Israelis to use in humiliating the Palestinians? That the country that invented the light bulb and powered flight faked the moon landings to appropriate the crescent? I don't think so. Most of the Hejazis I knew engaged in such rash talk as something of a parlor game. It soothed their troubled, and insecure, souls. More important, because ridiculous conspiracy theories were (and are) the stock-in-trade of Middle Eastern "journalists," almost invariably with the blessings of their regimes, my contacts felt they had license to castigate the United States. Most would much rather have complained about their own governments, and some did. But this could be a perilous undertaking. By attacking America, the sole superpower and Saudi Arabia's most prominent Western partner, my Saudi friends could feel safe and, in some small way, get their licks in on the Al Saud, too.

The terrorist attacks of September 11, 2001, demonstrated nothing if not that the Al Saud exercised far less influence, not to mention control, over its subjects than senior princes—or anyone else—believed. Jeddah's parlor-game anti-Americans were horrified to learn that there were people who truly believed the inanities they drolly trotted out each night over hookahs and sweet tea. Few urban Hejazi elites were prepared to acknowledge that a significant, even overwhelming, percentage of ordinary Saudis accepted the mosques' view that the atrocities represented the hand of a vengeful God punishing America for its impudence. None had foreseen that two decades' enforcement of suffocatingly strict Islamic behavior, a faltering economy, a youthful and idle population, virtually unlimited funds channeled toward inculcating Wahhabism, and tacit official encouragement to hate the West would combine to produce a toxic tea no Saudi can credibly claim not to have sipped, with al-Qa'ida's deadly operations in the Kingdom beginning in 2003 the bitter aftertaste.

During my three years reporting on developments in western Saudi Arabia, I often wondered whether the Hejaz was approaching dusk or dawn. Would this storied land of faith and of commerce, this vital portal between East and West, continue to decline along with the rest of the Kingdom? How much remains of its once-distinct identity? Could it stand on its own after eight decades of Saudi overlordship? The answers, of course, will depend on the courage and desires of the Hejazis themselves. For now, however, it is twilight in the Hejaz. In this place whose Arabic name refers to its being bounded by the mountains and the sea, time—like twilight itself—seems forever suspended between day and night, darkness and light, yesterday and tomorrow.

CHAPTER 1
Life and Death

Life is pleasant. Death is peaceful. It's the transition that's troublesome.

—Isaac Asimov

I started my inquiries into the Saudi reality by focusing on the two constants of western Arabia, life and death. I wanted to grasp the importance Hejazis placed on the stages of existence, from birth, through marriage, and on to eternity. In so doing, I discovered that such examinations were impossible in a vacuum; Arabs have, since time immemorial, survived in some of the planet's harshest environments only because they forged enduring relationships with the rest of world. The degree to which the insular occupants of the Peninsula (whose Arabic name, *al-Jazirah,* is synonymous with "island") welcomed or repelled outsiders tracked closely with the fortunes of a land that, for much of the millennia since the last ice age, has had more than a passing acquaintance with poverty, pestilence, and privation.

The engagement of a Saudi friend to his childhood sweetheart prompted me to look into the institution of marriage, the subject of the first report in this chapter. What I found had less to do with love and commitment than with family honor and, in some cases, greed. The connubial arrangements and maneuvering I found also served to highlight the status, or, more accurately, the lack thereof, accorded women in the Hejaz. More than 14 centuries after the Prophet Muhammad declared an end to the treatment of females as chattel, the fact remains that, even today, women in the land of his birth rarely control their own fates. As with some terrorized slaves in the antebellum South who felt secure in a predictable, paternal cocoon and therefore defended the "peculiar institution" because they could not envision a different way of life, so too do many Saudi women condemn Western fretting about their treatment as motivated less by a genuine concern for human rights than by the supposed age-old desire of outsiders—particularly Christians and "Zionists"—to impugn local tradition and thereby rend the fabric of a society purportedly modeled more closely than any other on Islamic precepts.

Death is the subject of the second report in this chapter. Muslims in the Hejaz generally die peacefully and, within 24 hours, are planted in the ground to await the Day of Judgment. Non-Muslims frequently are not so fortunate. A fair number experience violent ends, which these days often involve traffic accidents.[1] In previous eras, many of those intrepid enough to make it to the Hejaz succumbed to disease, dehydration, or disembowelment at the hands of locals, some of whom to this day look upon foreigners as mere vessels bearing riches a callous and capricious God has seen fit to deny his most faithful servants. One stifling summer afternoon, I visited Jeddah's little-known non-Muslim cemetery (NMC), the final resting place of some of the Hejaz's more misfortunate visitors. Frequented less often by mourners than by vandals and vigilantes intent on obliterating any suggestion there might be valid spiritual paths other than that prescribed by Islam, it is a haunting, melancholy place that—despite lying beneath a scorching sun—chilled me to the bone.

No discussion of existence in the Hejaz would be complete without mention of its life's blood, trade. Before the advent of Christianity, the region prospered by taking advantage of Rome's growing desire for spices and the East's need to support its swelling populations. Hejazis thus first achieved global prominence as middlemen and traders par excellence, generating a pride for which they ever since have appeared to pay. The collapse of the spice trade in the Christian era was preceded by maritime advances that enabled commerce to bypass the increasingly predatory Peninsula traders. The subsequent, explosive spread from Arabia of a new, global faith—Islam—proved less a blessing than a curse in the lives of many Hejazis. For as the pilgrim trade restored revenues, it also attracted the attention of outsiders, far and near. These outsiders would seek to mold the Muslim holy land in ways that served the ends, not of God, but of kings.

Marriage, Money, and Men of Modest Means (May 2000)

If marriage is the foundation of this society, then its apotheosis is realized in the generation of sons. Births among Saudis are occasions fraught with great anticipation. The father-to-be endures near-constant reminders from friends and relations that he must sire a son to prove his manhood and secure his lineage. The expectation that the child be a boy falls even more heavily on the mother. Despite what is now known about how a baby's sex is determined, it is the woman who usually is blamed for not producing a son. Indeed, the arrival of a daughter sometimes is occasioned by grieving so intense that an outsider might be forgiven for believing a member of the family had died.

Infanticide having been outlawed under Islam, female babies in the Hejaz usually reach maturity as members of their father's household. Their value, however, is regarded as negative before they marry. Until such time, their actions carry the potential of bringing dishonor on their families and so they are kept safely sequestered from public life. A girl's potential worth is achieved once she reaches a marriageable age, generally 12 and up, depending on where in the Hejaz she resides. The father realizes his reward for having raised a chaste daughter in the *maher*—the dowry or bride price her hand can command. Although, in theory, the entire dowry is supposed to go to the bride to ensure that she has assets not subject to her husband's control, in practice, brides' fathers frequently retain a hefty percentage, and sometimes all, of the bride-price. Once a suitable match is made, the father names his figure. It is presented to the would-be groom's family as a nonnegotiable proposition. For centuries, fathers have felt compelled to set a price that is high enough to reflect honorably on his household and the virtue of its women.

Unfortunately, the decline in Hejazi living standards in recent years means that many grooms' families cannot afford current bride-prices. Moreover, honor considerations will not permit a girl's father to reduce his dowry demand to make it easier on the boy's father. The calculus runs something like this: "What will the neighbors think of my daughter if I ask less for her hand than I did for her older sister's? How will people regard my household if I am perceived as a father so anxious to marry off his daughter that he does it on the cheap?" These are serious considerations in a society in which image, particularly within the status-conscious and economically squeezed middleclass, can mean the difference between upward mobility and a rapid descent into social and financial ignominy. Enter the Islamic Affairs Ministry and at least two Muslim charities with a solution: financial aid to help grooms' fathers pay the dowries.

I spoke recently with an official from the World Assembly of Muslim Youth (WAMY), who explained how his organization assists grooms' fathers in paying the bride-price. He said that the Islamic Affairs Ministry and the Al-Haramayn Foundation—another Saudi enterprise ostensibly dedicated to charitable pursuits—undertake similar efforts. WAMY's program, he claimed, is the most venerable, having provided dowry assistance since 1992.

According to the official, WAMY helps pay an average of 5,000 dowries each year throughout Saudi Arabia. In Jeddah, the organization helped some 850 grooms get married during the Islamic year 1420 (which ended on April 4, 2000). The average amount of assistance provided to the grooms' fathers was 30,000 riyals ($8,000). In most cases, he said, this covered the entire bride-price. However, at least a third of the time, and particularly in urban areas like Jeddah and Mecca, WAMY's assistance covers only part of what the bride's father demands of the groom's. Dowries, which were much more modest before the oil-boom years, have continued to climb, while Saudi incomes have not, he lamented.

To bankroll its bride-price program, WAMY uses funds it receives from the Saudi government as well as money it collects from the public via collection boxes placed in front of stores and from the sale of sermons on cassette tapes. To be eligible for assistance, the fathers of prospective grooms must have received a specific dowry demand from the bride's father, the receipt of which functions as the de facto acceptance of the groom's family's marriage proposal. The groom's father must then appear before a committee composed of three members of WAMY's board of directors and demonstrate that he requires financial aid to pay part or all of the bride-price. According to the WAMY official, this usually is done by producing bank or paycheck receipts, a description of his home and the number of wives and children, and a list of debts. Al-Haramayn operates along similar lines, but the Ministry (whose program is the newest) makes grants in response to written applications. There is no expectation on the part of the charities or the Ministry that men seeking dowry assistance first exhaust other potential sources of financial aid, such as family and friends.

WAMY and al-Haramayn do not provide dowry assistance to older men seeking to marry young women, particularly as second, third, or fourth wives, the official said. Although the charities focus solely on helping fathers with sons entering their first marriages, the Ministry will aid aging spouse-seekers. WAMY also differs from al-Haramayn and the Ministry in that it neither attempts to arrange marriages nor encourages group weddings as a means of further reducing expenditures. According to the WAMY official, al-Haramayn has played host to one group wedding in Mecca so far this Islamic year (1421), while the Ministry announced last month (in April 2000) that it aims to collect 10 million riyals ($2.67 million) to help 1,000 young Saudi men get married this summer (in summer 2000). In addition to forming a partnership with al-Rajhi Bank to solicit donations for this endeavor, the Ministry has launched a Web site providing information on its service and how one may contribute (www.alzawaj.org).

At WAMY's insistence, I was invited by the father of a Saudi groom to attend his son's wedding on May 4, 2000. The men's portion of the event took place at an outdoor lot adjacent to a party hall in the lower-middleclass al-Rawabi District of southeast Jeddah. In the stifling heat of a windless evening, I sat on cheap, machine-made carpets with approximately 70 of the groom's male family members and friends. Mint tea was served, and some of the guests made idle conversation. Most, however, lounged silently in an atmosphere that was more contractual than nuptial. Meanwhile, the sound of thumping music and whooping women's voices could be heard coming from the hall next door as the bride's female relatives and friends celebrated. After an hour or so, the groom and his father appeared to greet their guests. More tea followed perfunctory handshakes and kisses. Then a tribal elder in a dusty shift appeared to read an ode in honor of the occasion.

The ode, delivered in a drawling dialect which I could barely follow, extolled the prowess of the tribe—the al-Jumayh—with which the groom's family identified, glorifying the deeds of its men and flower of its youth as epitomized by the groom. My neighbor on the carpets, an older cousin of the groom, said that the tribal elder made his living reciting at weddings, births, and other celebrations. His usual fee is 2,500 riyals ($667); the cousin said the groom's unemployed father, with WAMY's help, persuaded the old man to accept 1,250 riyals. The cousin further confided that the groom's father was mortified lest I learn how much assistance WAMY was providing; the charity paid the entire dowry: 36,000 riyals ($9,600).

Following the ode, the groom and his father were escorted by the bride's father and brothers into the hall, which erupted into an otherworldly din of ululation. The embarrassed-looking pair reappeared outside 20 minutes later, the signal for the male guests—led by the tribal elder—to rush toward several long tables where roast lamb, rice, bread, pickled vegetables, and fruit were piled in abundance.[2] I learned from the groom's cousin that the feast was provided by former coworkers of the groom's father, who had lost his job at a paint factory because of absenteeism occasioned by an unspecified industrial accident. The guests departed immediately after the feeding frenzy; the entire production had lasted approximately two-and-one-half hours. The groom subsequently was taken to his bride's family's home for pictures (paid for out of the dowry), then back to his father's house, where the couple will reside until they find a home of their own. The groom is newly employed as a clerk at the Jeddah Islamic Port.

Dowry assistance provided by charities to grooms' fathers (and, in the case of the Ministry, to older husbands-to-be) is criticized by a fair number of people in the Hejaz. Many of those who see these programs as wrongheaded are self-described modern Hejazi women, but some are forward-thinking men. These men and women complain that by financing the payment of high bride-prices, the charities and the Ministry are making it increasingly difficult for older, well-educated, divorced, and widowed Saudi women to get married.

At least one press report supports these views. An article in the London-based Arabic daily *Al-Sharq al-Awsat* on April 11, 2000, claimed that one-third of Saudi females are at risk of becoming spinsters, with high dowries cited as a contributing factor. According to the Planning Ministry, there are 1,529,418 unmarried women in Saudi Arabia. Mecca has the highest number (396,248), followed by Riyadh (327,427) and the Eastern Province (228,093). The Planning Ministry published in the local papers what it termed a clarification on May 8, 2000, stating that no more than 2 percent of Saudi women of marriageable age remained unmarried. Nonetheless, the original, alarming statistics have stoked a firestorm of controversy in the Hejaz. Traditional Hejazi matchmakers report business is booming as they attempt to find husbands for women whose families fear are at risk for spinsterhood.[3]

A stay-at-home Saudi mother told me in April 2000 that she is worried about what will happen if her niece, currently studying for a master's degree in the United States, fails to attract a husband of means upon her return to the Kingdom. She explained that Saudi men are intimidated by smart women. Her brother, the girl's father, might be forced to seek a lower dowry to prevent his daughter from becoming a spinster. However, by enabling less-than-wealthy men to pay higher dowries, WAMY and other organizations increase the disincentive for a Saudi boy to marry a well-educated girl. In other words, if a boy's father receives assistance allowing him to meet whatever bride-price is demanded, the stay-at-home mom asked rhetorically, why shouldn't a boy look for a "stupid village girl who will never challenge him?" Instead of helping grooms' fathers pay high dowries, she continued, the Islamic Affairs Ministry and charities like WAMY should use their influence to convince brides' fathers to face economic reality and make reasonable demands.

On May 2, 2000, the native Jeddawi manager of a local travel and tourism company told me that he believed dowry assistance programs distorted what had been a well-balanced marriage system in the Hejaz. Polygamy, he said, traditionally enabled widows and divorced women to find new partners and live dignified lives. With older men receiving help from the Ministry to meet high bride-prices, they are able to take young girls, who previously were out of reach, as second, third, or fourth wives. They no longer want to "settle for shopworn merchandise." The result is that financially strapped fathers of young girls, finding themselves in a seller's market, are marrying their daughters off to the highest bidders instead of pausing to consider whether potential sons-in-law are suitable matches. From their perspective, if suitors from top-drawer clans fail to materialize, would-be husbands from less-affluent families that have received dowry assistance will apply; a no-lose proposition. The travel company manager concluded that WAMY, al-Haramayn, and the Islamic Affairs Ministry tried to do good but wound up creating a monster.

Flowers for Ousman (June 2000)

Although non-Muslims in Jeddah risk arrest by practicing their religions openly, more than 400 deceased non-Muslims, including at least 13 Americans, rest in peace beneath the symbols of their faiths in the city's Non-Muslim Cemetery (NMC), the only one of its kind in Saudi Arabia. The first reference to it appears in an account Danish explorer Carsten Niebuhr wrote of his expedition to Yemen. On his way to what the Romans termed Arabia Felix in 1762, Niebuhr visited Jeddah and sketched a plan of the city. It shows a "Christian cemetery" outside the town wall to the south, in a position at or near the present NMC.[4]

Jeddawis, acting in accordance with a diplomatic agreement established during the era of Ottoman rule, looked after the NMC in its early years. When Jeddah was surrendered to the Wahhabis in 1925, the graveyard was vandalized and, eventually, ignored—at least by local Muslims. Non-Muslims continued to bury their indigent and eccentric dead there. During 1991–94, a committee composed of representatives from the consulates whose nationals used the cemetery held a series of meetings with an eye toward refurbishing the NMC, which had fallen into serious disrepair. At the committee's behest, a contractor engaged by the German Consulate began work in early 1995.

The renovation, which cost approximately 350,000 riyals ($93,333), was financed through donations from consulates, expatriate business groups, and various individuals. The wall surrounding the NMC was repaired and repainted and the old wooden entrance was replaced with a stone structure. The cemetery was made level; this required up to 40 centimeters of fill in some places. The original, crumbling concrete gravestones were replaced with new ones made of marble, and several old cenotaphs were cleaned. Walkways were installed, and trees, vines, and other vegetation were planted. A small office and living quarters for the caretaker—including a kitchen and bathroom—were constructed. Finally, the layout of existing graves was altered to maximize the usable space within the NMC, with some of the more historically significant monuments moved to new sites along the western wall.

To provide funding for a contract gardening company to maintain the grounds and to pay the caretaker's salary, the burial fee was raised from 1,500 riyals ($400) to 2,500 riyals ($666.67) in late 1995. There have been at least 20 burials since (mainly of Filipinos, Eritreans, and Indians), and as a result the NMC—with more than 400 graves—has reached maximum capacity. According to the Dutch Consul General, there may be room for the interment of one or two infants, but an adult-size coffin would be a tight squeeze. On behalf of the committee consulates, the Dutch in April 2000 submitted to the Foreign Ministry a request for another plot of land on which to establish a new non-Muslim cemetery. There has been no official response to date, but Ministry contacts told me that Foreign Minister Saud al-Faysal is favorably disposed toward the request.

Among the NMC's more notable residents is French explorer Charles Huber, who was born in Strasbourg on December 19, 1847, and died in the Hejaz on July 29, 1884. Huber was known as the discoverer of the Tayma Stone, a 1.10-meter-tall, 150-kg sandstone stela, inscribed in Aramaic, which shed light on the early history of the Hejaz.[5] Huber's gray stone sarcophagus is among the oldest surviving monuments in the NMC, but there is some question as to whether Huber's remains are inside. The explorer was murdered by his local guides somewhere between Jeddah and Mecca, after which his body remained exposed for some days before being buried by passersby.

According to the Strasbourg municipal archives as researched by the British consul there in 1954, Huber's remains were transferred to the

NMC by his associate, an Algerian exile named Sidi Aziz ibn Shaykh al-Haddad. Sidi Aziz subsequently acquired possession of the Tayma Stone from the Amir of Ha'il, Muhammad ibn Rashid—whom Huber had entrusted with its safekeeping—and sent it to the Louvre. At the time of Huber's re-interment by Sidi Aziz, his skeleton reportedly was complete, except that his hands were missing. A bullet hole was found near the left temple. On page 243 of his book *Christians at Mecca* (London: Heinemann, 1909), Augustus Ralli wrote that Huber's skull was buried in Jeddah but the rest of his remains (except for the hands, which were never recovered) were spirited out of the Hejaz in 1885 by Dutch Islamic scholar C. Snouck Hugronje (who, in the guise of a Muslim convert named Abd al-Ghaffar, made some of the earliest photographs of Mecca). No other accounts support this claim.

Cyril Ousman, the British vice consul whom Prince Mishari bin Abd al-Aziz Al Saud shot and killed in a drunken rage in Jeddah in 1951 after Ousman had the audacity to refuse Mishari another drink—the event that precipitated the banning of alcohol in the Kingdom—also reposes at the NMC. (Mishari died in the United States on May 23, 2000, following what press reports characterized as a long illness. In keeping with royal family custom, he was buried in an unmarked grave in the desert outside Riyadh.) Ousman's prerenovation gravestone stated that he was born on October 6, 1903, and that he died on November 16, 1951. It further indicated that he posthumously was made a Member of the British Empire. His 1995-issue marker, like all the cemetery's new gravestones, omits all information except his name.

I visited the NMC on one cloudless, blistering hot afternoon in June. The hectare-size site lies in the middle of a dense commercial and residential district in southwest Jeddah. Apartment buildings overlook the northern and western sides, while an elevated freeway roars just beyond the cemetery's southern flank. The work completed in 1995 held up reasonably well, with the wall, the walkways, and the new gate and caretaker's quarters clean and in good repair. Except for the trees, the vegetation planted five years earlier had died.

A walk among the graves revealed the sad fact that more than one-third of the interments—up to and including the most recent—were of infants who did not survive childbirth. A number of these and other graves, particularly those of Filipinos, bore evidence (flowers, candles, candies, and plush toys) of recent visitation. Huber's sarcophagus, meanwhile, now lies along the western wall. In the old NMC configuration, his head pointed east; it now points north. I placed a bouquet on Ousman's final resting place, which is near the northeastern corner.

The Life of Spice (December 2000)

Among Saudi Arabia's five administrative regions (northern, western, southern, eastern, and central), the western is the least insular. It has a fundamentally outward-looking orientation that derives in part from its location along a key sector of the ancient spice route. From its inception some 3,000 years ago, the overland trade featured frankincense from Oman and gum arabic from Yemen. Subsequent merchant activities meant that caravans along the well-worn paths leading north to the Roman Empire's Levantine possessions included myrrh from Persia, sandalwood from Indonesia, and a host of spices from the Indus Valley and from as far away as China.

The main trade route followed the coastal plain of western Arabia from the Yemeni mountains north to the Gulf of Aqaba. This narrow (200 miles at its widest), approximately 750-mile-long corridor of rocky crags and desolate desert dotted with date palms became known as the Hejaz, meaning "separating," a reference to the escarpment dividing it from the plateau to the east. The name also connotes "set aside" or "reserved." The towns that sprang up along the spice route through the Hejaz reached agreements with the surrounding nomadic tribes concerning the protocol of plunder. Random raids on the caravans were to be avoided in favor of predatory commercial practices and various safe-passage levies amounting to a protection racket.

Rome's adoption of Christianity resulted in a steep decline in cremations as well as in the number of gods worshipped in the empire and, thus, in the amount of incense needed for burnt offerings. Concomitant maritime advances enabled merchants to transport spices and other goods more quickly and cheaply by sea. By the time of the Prophet Muhammad in the seventh century, the spice route was carrying a mere trickle of the commerce it once had witnessed. The Hejaz, like Oman and Yemen before it, appeared destined to drift into obscurity.

However, long before the coming of Islam and the spice route's demise, savvy merchants in several Hejazi towns hit upon the idea of attracting caravansary and enticing them to stay for longer periods by hosting festivals. Defying the general intolerance of the age, they invited traders to bring symbols of their gods with them (in pre-Islamic times, nomadic tribes traveled with portable stone idols) and allowed these to be displayed for the duration of the festivities. Recognizing that too many celebrations would dilute their overall effectiveness, the merchants began to hold them only once each lunar year.[6] Ultimately, the various festivals were consolidated into a single event held in the baking Bakka Valley east of Jeddah. An old temple was refurbished to permanently display more than 300 tribal idols, thus guaranteeing the traders would return annually as pilgrims. This temple was called the Kaaba. The town that developed around it to service the pilgrimage trade became known as Mecca.

There were other religious attractions in the Hejaz and along the spice route. Jeddah successfully lured credulous Christians and Jews (and, later, Muslims) for centuries with a large shrine reputed to be Eve's tomb. In Najran, several hundred kilometers southeast of Mecca, a rival Kaaba at Jabal Taslal drew worshippers for some 40 years during the pre-Islamic era. However, no place rivaled Mecca for the sheer size, spectacle, and notoriety of its annual festival. Pilgrims and traders were feted with wine, women, and song, and most left with coin purses that were considerably lighter than when they arrived. As the city prospered, so did the region. Hejazis had turned their tolerance of different customs and beliefs to commercial advantage, a skill that would serve them well following the advent of Islam.

By Muhammad's time, the people of the Hejaz were a fairly well-assimilated polyglot of different races and creeds. African, Persian, and Greek minorities lived side by side and sometimes intermarried with indigenous folk and new arrivals from South Arabia. Christians and Jews mingled with animists, Sabeans, and Zoroastrians. Although one's lineage was (and is) important in determining the social pecking order in the Hejaz, business prowess was (and remains) the *sine qua non* of economic status. Because nearly every enterprise depended directly or indirectly on revenues from the pilgrimage to Mecca, the hajj became the region's commercial lodestar.

The Prophet's goal of purifying what he believed to be the original house of Allah posed a direct threat to the Hejazi way of life. What, locals may have asked themselves, will attract pilgrims here if the totems are removed from the Kaaba? Muhammad's faith, founded on the proposition that there is no deity but Allah (a grumpy-seeming god who rejected idols even in his own name), clearly could not be tolerated. A standoff ensued until the preeminent Hejazi tribe of the time, the Quraysh, recognized—under some duress—that Islam was winning large numbers of devout adherents who literally were lining up to worship in Mecca. Astute enough to flow with a tide that had turned, and, perhaps, recognizing the economic boost Muhammad and his followers previously had given Medina to the north, the Quraysh and their allies capitulated and handed the Kaaba over to the Muslims. Far from throwing a wet blanket on the hajj and the businesses that depended on it, Islam provided the spark of perpetual life. A funky regional festival was transformed overnight into one of the five pillars of the world's fastest-growing faith.

Although the Muslims' temporal capital was moved from the Hejaz shortly after the Prophet's death, the region retained its identity as Islam's spiritual home. It grew steadily more prosperous and more diverse. As the faith spread, pilgrims from Andalusia, Africa, the Caucasus, and the subcontinent began arriving in large numbers to perform the hajj. Some, of course, stayed on, imbuing the local culture with an even greater awareness of the Hejaz's role as the center of gravity for the new, global religion.

Unfortunately, this awareness frequently was translated into ingenious schemes for fleecing pilgrims. All manner of Muslims, including the most heterodox of sects, were welcome to come, the sole admission requirement being the visitors' ability to pay for an ever-expanding array of supposedly indispensable gimcrackery. In acknowledging the importance of the pilgrimage to their way of life, locals referred to their guests as "the bread of the Hejaz" and to themselves as "God's neighbors." Pilgrims, remarking on the contrast between the exceptionally solicitous service they received before hajj (when they were flush with cash) and the shabby treatment meted out to them after its conclusion (when many were broke and stranded), often disparaged their hosts as "the dogs of the Hejaz."

The Hejaz's religious importance meant that it was regarded as an essential, if remote and relatively trouble-free, part of the Islamic caliphate. After 1269, it fell under the nominal rule of the Egyptian Mamelukes. The Ottomans gained control of it when they conquered Egypt in 1517.[7]

The region generally was equated with orthodox Sunni beliefs and practices, but its inhabitants included Muslims of every stripe, with Sufis (in Jeddah) and Shia (in Medina) particularly prevalent. To assist their citizens undertaking the pilgrimage, earth's greatest annual mass migration of human beings, Muslim countries began staffing diplomatic outposts in the Hejaz. Jeddah, as the major port on the Arabian side of the Red Sea, was the favored location. Soon, a number of non-Islamic states that had acquired Muslim colonial possessions also opened consulates. These included the Netherlands (Indonesia), Great Britain (India), and France (North Africa). Of course, these consulates did more than merely look after the welfare of pilgrims.

In the run-up to World War I, the Hejaz was viewed by the Great Powers as a vulnerable and potentially detachable portion of the

Ottoman Empire. Possession of it—through proxy, if not outright—might prove useful to a colonial master interested in retaining or acquiring influence in Muslim lands. Russia, Germany, and Italy soon opened their own consulates in Jeddah. Locals, reveling in Europe's newfound interest in their region, began referring to the Hejaz in general and Jeddah in particular as the "land of the consuls." Independence, a western concept that had not meant much in a place traditionally left to its own devices, became important to residents annoyed at Istanbul's increasingly heavy-handed attempts to regulate the hajj. Seeds of change began to sprout in the Hejaz.

The Great War irrevocably changed two elements of the Hejazi identity. First, thanks to Britain's Near Eastern intrigues augmented by T.E. Lawrence's Arab Revolt, locals were encouraged to regard themselves as a distinct people possessing a viable and geographically defined homeland. The Hejaz had ceased to exist as merely a mental construct or a romantic fiction; it had become a political reality. Husayn, the Hashemite Sharif of Mecca, declared the Kingdom of the Hejaz (with himself, of course, as king) in 1915.

Second, the dismembering of the Ottoman octopus enabled Hejazis to consider the possibility that their region could again become Islam's temporal as well as spiritual home. Many scoffed at Husayn's desire to become caliph and personally lead a pan-Islamic revival, but only because the man—not the mission—seemed inappropriate. Having thrown off the yoke of the Turks, Hejazis were disgusted by Hussein's pretensions, regarding him as simply a more proximate, and no less corrupt, emblem of the *ancien régime*. A rickety state bureaucracy struggled to rebuild a pilgrimage that was devastated by years of war and strife, while the king went about depleting what remained of the British-endowed treasury in pursuit of feckless stratagems aimed at convincing Islamic leaders of the legitimacy of his claim to the mantle of the Prophet. Small wonder, then, that the unlettered Wahhabi legions of King Abd al-Aziz Al Saud (known in the West as Ibn Saud) were welcomed by some Hejazis as liberators in 1924–25. Less surprising is that liberty was not quite what the conquerors from the Najd (central Arabia) had in mind.

Al Saud rule of the Hejaz began on a deceptively light note. Jeddah was declared the diplomatic capital of the new Kingdom of the Hejaz and Najd (becoming the Kingdom of Saudi Arabia in 1932, following additional conquests, particularly in the south). In a tacit admission of the western region's superior educational development, Hejazi teachers were recruited in large numbers to staff schools in the central region.

The 1925 hajj was the first conducted under Ibn Saud's supervision, and he decreed an end to the bacchanalia that characterized local *eid* (feast) celebrations and ordered the region's merchants to stop ripping off God's supplicants. In the following few years, life went on as before for most residents. Although the Wahhabis patrolled the streets forcing shops to close for prayer and men to attend the mosques, local forms of dress (white turban and tan shift for men, brightly embroidered gowns and face covers for women) were tolerated, men and women were not segregated in public places, Sufis and Shia were not overtly harassed, and the hajj witnessed a renaissance as pilgrims recognized it had become a more secure, and sober, family-oriented event.

In the 1930s and 1940s, however, attempts by the Al Saud to exercise tighter control over what was sometimes viewed as a frontier of fickle fealty resulted in a gradual homogenization of the Hejaz. Fear of the region's extensive contacts with the Muslim and non-Muslim world at large led the authorities to regulate commercial transactions and communications. Najdi *amirs* (rulers) were installed to oversee these activities, and the customs they brought with them influenced would-be local courtiers. Hejazis on the make adopted the *thobe* (white, ankle-length gown) and *ghutra* (Bedouin headdress) and aped the Al Saud's guttural dialect. Schools began inculcating a Saudi version of history along with the xenophobic Wahhabi ethos, and the practice of other forms of Islam was forcefully discouraged. Music and alcohol were enjoined, card and backgammon parlors closed, and segregation of the sexes imposed. Observances of the *mawlid* (Muhammad's birthday, long a major feast day in the Hejaz) were banned. Hajj-related fees that previously went into the sharif's coffers now were siphoned off to build palaces in Riyadh.

Like the rest of Arabia, the Hejaz experienced a number of lean years during the Great Depression and World War II, when the flow of pilgrims virtually ceased. As the 1950s dawned, things brightened considerably, with the hajj rebounding and oil revenues beginning to fatten people's pocketbooks. By the 1960s, the Hejaz had become an integral part of the Al Saud's puritanical peninsular empire. Through the ensuing decades, the region's culture became progressively less distinguishable from that of the central region and, indeed, from that of the other Persian Gulf countries. Although profits from the pilgrimage provided residents with some insulation from Riyadh's use of employment and largesse to purchase political quiescence, most Hejazis needed little encouragement to embrace the new era of consumerism engendered by the petrodollar windfall.

Only after the oil market bottomed out in the late 1980s did Hejazis begin to question whether they had moved too quickly to exchange their Hejazi-ness for what increasingly appeared to be an artificial and bankrupt national identity. Why, some asked, were archeologically significant sites that did not conform with the Wahhabi version of history (both pre- and post-Islam) desecrated or obliterated? Are the Najdis' narrow views really morally superior to our sloppy old tolerance? Do the Al Saud, or any of the tribes affiliated with them, have the right to extract money from the western region and spend it elsewhere? Do we not have our own history, our own heroes, our own values that are distinctly not of the Najd or of the Gulf? Are we not the true heirs of the Prophet and the Islamic civilization that he founded here?

In point of fact, the people asking such questions belong to the older generations that retain memories of times past. Local youth, by contrast, seem unable to verbalize such sentiments. They are stifled by the region's cultural homogenization and only dimly aware of its free-wheeling, pilgrim-fleecing past. But instead of wringing their hands and pining for days gone by, some are forging a new self-concept they hope will lead to a brighter future.

These young people reflect the region's traditions as well as the dramatic changes it has undergone since the end of World War II. As a result, they sometimes seem to have contradictory natures: They are conservative and action-oriented; repressed and curious; they value family and individuality; they want to be in the world while resisting its influences; they want to be taken care of while insisting on having a say. More street-smart and less idealistic than their parents and grandparents, they are evolutionaries, not revolutionaries, who recognize that their region's fortunes are inexorably linked to a national, Saudi polity. At the same time, their desire to distinguish themselves from fellow citizens elsewhere may impel them to address their elders' concerns by taking an interest in preserving and, perhaps, celebrating the unique history that makes them Hejazis.

CHAPTER 2
Holy Cities

There is no need for temples, no need for compli-
cated philosophies. My brain and my heart are
my temples; my philosophy is kindness.
                                                    —Dalai Lama

Saudis see themselves as lacking entertainment opportunities. Their
vast country—about the size of the United States east of the
Mississippi—contains no Disneyland, no Colonial Williamsburg, not
even a NASCAR-like venue. One consequence of the Kingdom's
paucity of diversions is the summertime exodus of Saudis with means
for months-long vacations in Europe and the United States.[1] Another
is the popularity, particularly among less well-heeled Saudis, of the
Hejazi cities of Jeddah, Mecca, and Medina. For many, an annual trip
to the holy cities, preceded or followed by several days' shopping,
noshing, and strolling along the shore in Jeddah, is the highlight of an
otherwise desperately dull existence.

Jeddah's political and business leaders have attempted to capitalize
on the internal tourism trade by promoting their city with an annual
summer festival. Featuring events such as Royal Saudi Air Force stunt
shows, exhibitions of art and fashion at local malls, and raffles and
giveaways at upscale hotels, the festival has proven an effective means
of filling the city with non-Hejazis during the interminably hot summer
months; occupancy rates at the Sheraton, Hilton, and Intercontinental
routinely average 90 percent or better from June through August. As

for the winter months, each year since 1999 Jeddah has played host to an economic forum at which global leaders (including former Presidents George H.W. Bush and Bill Clinton, keynote speakers in 2000 and 2002, respectively) discuss the region's commercial prospects. The message, both explicit and implicit, is that the Hejaz is headed for a bright future.

While such endeavors are intended to point the way forward, they invariable left me wondering what the zeal to build a shining, progressive Hejaz said about the cities and peoples who presumably were to be modernized. I discovered that Saudis, far from being reverent toward their past, were blindly determined to give anything that smacked of pre-petrodollar affluence the boot. Like immigrants to the United States in the early twentieth century who saw assimilation as the way up the economic ladder and thus did not discuss the lives they left behind—much less teach their mother tongues to their children—so, too, do Saudis in the Hejaz appear embarrassed by the relics around them, bespeaking a time before money made conveniences like air conditioning and automobiles possible.

The Saudis I knew lived in terror of the thought that the Westerner, mythologized as a character of utmost advancement and discernment (albeit uncouth and lacking the moral fiber of Islam), would look upon them patronizingly as arrivistes in the modern world. Thus, the traditional, multistory, coral-block-and-timber homes in which generations of merchants had raised their families in the teeming heart of Jeddah's old city were to be kept from the Westerner's view (or, better yet, demolished). Westerners were to be received and feted in the new concrete mansions with their marble floors, rococo furniture, and expansive, green gardens. No expense would be spared to show them that to be a Saudi in the Hejaz was to be the equal, nay, the superior of the New Yorker, the Parisian, the Londoner; Saudi wealth and refinement were better because they were accompanied by Islam. In fact, today's urban Hejazis live in a fantasyland sustained by shame and a tragic inferiority complex, one in which they pantomime behaviors—from swilling Scotch to sporting Gucci loafers—they suppose will make them more Western. Meanwhile, the five-times-daily call to prayer, substituting for "It's a Small World After All," serves to underscore the impossibility of their escaping the fact that they come from a land in which a global faith arose and which is home to its two holiest cities.

Medina, the subject of the first report in this chapter, is the lesser of the two holy cities. Known before the coming of Islam as Yathrib, it was a tolerant, trade-oriented town featuring extensive date-palm plantations as well as sizeable, and powerful, Jewish clans. When the Prophet was forced to flee Mecca in the wake of its leaders' crackdown on what they viewed as a dangerous, revolutionary creed, Medina's citizens—impressed by Muhammad's humility and mediation skills (he frequently was called upon to settle inter-tribal disputes)—invited him and his followers to take refuge among them, earning for Medinans of the era the sobriquet *al-Ansar,* or the supporters of Islam. In a short time, the Prophet, far from keeping a low profile, had consolidated power in Medina and made of it the world's first Islamic city. Many residents willingly embraced the new faith, while others—notably the Jews—kept their own but sought tactical alliances with the Muslims.

In the crucible of conflict that ensued between the Meccans, guardians of the old tribal and pagan order, and Muhammad's Medinans, the Prophet honed his political skills and, eventually, succeeded in conquering Mecca and establishing Islam as the official religion of his Arabian empire. Unfortunately, Muhammad's military judgment appeared to be based more on faith than on common sense. In one storied incident, he failed to see to it that his archers maintained their positions during a critical battle, leading to a route in which he nearly lost his life. In another story that carries repercussions to this day, the Prophet assumed the Jews were strategic allies and was dismayed when some changed their allegiance as the Meccans appeared ascendant. Qur'anic verses revealed to Muhammad at this time castigate the Jews as untrustworthy backstabbers; these verses have been seized on by some latter-day zealots to justify anti-Semitism.[2]

Medina today is clean, orderly, and—by Saudi standards—a reasonably laid-back town. Set on a high plateau broken by vast, black lava flows from now-dormant volcanic fissures and canyons wherein agriculture has taken place along seasonal streams for millennia, the city shimmers with a peculiar light that seems to challenge the brooding, purple peaks defining its northern and eastern flanks.[3] A steady, mint-tinged northwesterly breeze serves to blow trash and cloud cover alike away, and the eponymous province for which it serves as the capital is an administrative proving ground for up-and-comers among the Kingdom's 15,000-odd princes.[4] Perhaps because the millions who visit the Prophet's tomb represent such an overt challenge to Wahhabi admonitions against anything smacking of idolatry, the Saudi official establishment by and large has appeared willing to accept a degree of heterodoxy in return for the commercial windfall generated by the city's most famous resident.

Mecca, treated in the second report of this chapter, is more than the sum of its parts. Scruffy, chaotic, and set in a suffocating, rocky valley with few resources beyond the miraculous, never-ending Zam-Zam spring, Islam's paramount holy city is, at first glance, a disappointment. During my initial visit in October 1999, I was able to undertake the *umra,* the so-called minor or off-season pilgrimage, in record time. The place was weirdly vacant; the throngs normally cramming the great plaza of the Grand Mosque—an expanse of white Italian marble buffed by the bare feet of billions of the faithful—were nowhere in evidence. In performing all the obligatory rituals with perhaps 1,000 fellow pilgrims that fall, I felt unfulfilled, unchallenged. I wondered whether the hajj, the defining experience of faith for many Muslims, really was the grueling episode about which I had read.

Several *umras* later I felt I knew Islam's holiest city and its rhythms. A morning trip to Mecca, 65 kilometers east of Jeddah, was easily accomplished. Jeddawis—residents of Jeddah—are well-known for being adept at timing the ebbs and flows of Mecca's crowds. I had convinced myself that, like any urban Hejazi worth his salt, I could undertake a trip to the city with a minimum of fuss, perform the requisite ceremonies, purchase lunch and a few trinkets, and be home in the bosom of my family by dinnertime. How wrong I was.

Mecca, I have come to realize, is less a destination than a journey. The city's underwhelming aspect—tumbledown apartments and bland hotels, sewage and offal, and ditches within which workers struggle to embed the latest telecommunications lines—all are secondary to the approach. God, so a famous Meccan saying goes, is in your soles. Undertaking my *umras,* even the one on the Night of Power and Destiny marking the zenith of the fasting month of Ramadan in November 2001—the scene of more than a million faithful staring beyond the Grand Mosque's stadium lights to glimpse what Muhammad, perhaps only apocryphally, experienced as the "lighting of the night sky as day"—did not prepare me for the overwhelming crush and tide of humanity that is the hajj proper.

Tunnels and tents, umbrellas and street urchins, barbers and bead-sellers—Mecca is a riot of color and confusion, of bad roads and worse food, all playing bit parts in the divine spectacle that is the Grand Mosque and its focal point, the Kaaba. A cube-shaped, black-draped, stone-block structure toward which Muslims orient their prayers, the Kaaba possesses an energy that seems to stem from its simple, unprepossessing presence. Rumors that it was once a Christian church are stoked by curious, curved low walls (which, seen from above, resemble the outline of a former nave) lying just beyond the building's northeastern flank. The famous Black Stone, a broken, basketball-size probable meteorite held together in a silver collar embedded in the Kaaba's eastern corner, predates Islam. According to Muslim lore, however, Muhammad—who deemed the structure the original temple dedicated to God and rebuilt by a succession of prophets from Adam to Abraham—allowed the stone's inclusion because of its peculiar legend. Held to originally have been pure white, the stone, hurled from the heavens by God, purportedly turned black upon contact with the sins of mankind. Kissing it is an act of contrition, symbolizing the pilgrim's recognition of his or her fallibility.

In all, however, the sites and sounds of Mecca are an affirmation. The place is, as a fellow pilgrim once told me, just as he dreamed it would be—except that he could not quite recall the dream. The hardships of saving for a trip to the holy city, of undertaking the journey, of enduring the rituals and the crowds; these experiences, these tick marks in time, are, to me, what make the city special. Being in the city cheapens it: Sudanese women beg in front of signs declaring that mendicants will be arrested; a Burger King in a sparkling tower across from the Grand Mosque gives pilgrims the chance to enjoy a Whopper while watching their fellows circumambulate the Kaaba several floors below; a Pakistani pilgrim washes soiled underwear in a sink full of holy water. In the mind's eye, Mecca shines most brightly in the distance. It reenters consciousness, becomes comprehensible again only after one's departure. In recognition of this, I spent considerable time in late 2001 and early 2002 exploring various pilgrim paths and peregrinations—the subject of the third, fourth, and fifth reports in this chapter—particularly the time-honored commercial corridors the Prophet Muhammad sanctioned as "official" routes to the hajj. In so doing I paid calls at each of the *mawaqeet,* points where pilgrims must assume a state of ritual purity wherein ablutions are made, special garments are donned, and prayers are offered. I believe I am one of but a few Americans ever to have visited all five.

Medina Yesterday and Today (January 2000)

A 15-minute drive southwest on King Fahd Street from Medina's airport leads one to Medina proper and the *haram* (Muslims-only) zone that encircles the Prophet's Mosque. With violet, egg-shaped Mt. Ohud looming serenely in the background, the City of the Prophet straddles several high, reasonably well-watered valleys studded with palm groves and laced with chaparral. Two billboards of Crown Prince Abdallah welcome visitors. The first, barely 5 kilometers past the airport, features a smiling Abdallah with an upraised arm above the message "we welcome you to the first home of Islam." The second, just inside the city limits, depicts a less exuberant-looking Crown Prince and text that reads "may your stay here by blessed and full of meaning."

Traffic into the *haram* intensifies as one draws close to the mosque, yet it flows much more smoothly than an average evening on Jeddah's snarled streets. My visit during January 4–5 coincided with the winding down of Ramadan revelry in Medina, with many of the devout having gone to Mecca to observe the last 10 days of the fasting month, particularly *Leylat al-Qadr*—the Night of Power and Destiny—the anniversary of Muhammad's receipt of the first Qur'anic revelations, which most Saudis observe on the twenty-seventh night of Ramadan. The sudden appearance of blocks of nearly identical 25-story hotel and apartment complexes signals that the city center has been reached. In contrast to the grimness of these towers, which my local driver referred to derisively as "the concrete forest," the floodlit Prophet's Mosque shines from amid its vast, surrounding marble piazza like polished alabaster.[5]

After checking into a suite on the eighteenth floor of one of the hotels overlooking the mosque, I descended to perform *maghrib* (sunset) prayers with tens of thousands of fellow worshippers. Entering the mosque, I followed a large crowd to the spiritual center of the structure past several cavernous prayer halls boasting indigo-and-ochre tilework and soaring, arched columns. There, beneath a homely green dome dating to the early years of Islam, is the Sacred Chamber comprising the rooms in which the Prophet and his family once lived and where Muhammad is entombed. Fenced off by an ornate, floor-to-ceiling lattice of gold-plated, wrought iron bars, the five-sided chamber with its small, opaque windows, dominates a rather narrow, and perpetually congested passageway, at the southern end of which is the *qibla* (direction of prayer). The chamber's presence is, in fact, not unlike that of a very large and imposing worshipper, forcing Muslims to squeeze in front of and to either side of it when praying. Owing to the Saudis' sensitivity to anything that hints of idolatry, it is studiously ignored during supplications but becomes again the focal point of the mosque once prayers are concluded. Unlike the Kaaba—the cube-shaped stone structure at the center of Mecca's Grand Mosque—the Sacred Chamber is not surrounded by a phalanx of security men ready to clout with truncheons those overcome by untoward paroxysms of passion. Instead, members of the Kingdom's official clerical establishment stand watch largely, it appeared, in an effort to ensure that Shia did not pollute the premises with what Wahhabis regard as their blasphemous devotions.

Following prayers, the faithful streamed out of the mosque and into the surrounding plaza for fast-breaking picnics. I was invited by a group of Yemeni men to share their simple meal of grilled chicken, rice, and cucumber salad, washed down with mango juice. The men recently had come from Mecca, where they performed *umra*, and said they would return in March for the hajj. Hailing from Hodeidah on the Yemeni coast west of Sanaa, they supported themselves and paid for their travels by selling handmade prayer beads and *miswak* sticks—fibrous twigs harvested from the desert-dwelling *siwak* tree that Arabs have used for millennia as a combination toothbrush and dentifrice. The *miswak* business is good during Ramadan, noted the Yemenis, because Muslims are permitted to chew the sticks while fasting, thus somewhat satisfying their cravings for food and cigarettes. The appearance of at least 30 small, Zamboni-like polishing carts signaled the end of the picnic. An army of bright green-uniformed sanitation personnel—most of them obviously of Southeast Asian origin—began sweeping up and bagging trash and loading it onto the carts, which cruised back and forth buffing the marble pavers and spraying a lemon-scented disinfectant.

In what seemed an unconscious imitation of the *tawwaf*, or circumambulation of the Kaaba, the thousands of visitors simultaneously began a leisurely, counterclockwise stroll around the perimeter of the Prophet's Mosque. One full circuit took nearly half an hour to complete. Midway through the second revolution, I broke off and wandered through an adjacent souvenir market. Booth after booth of vendors, none of them staff by Saudis, offered everything from brass incense burners emblazoned with the royal family crest to snowglobe acrylic paperweights featuring miniature replicas of the Grand Mosque, the Prophet's Mosque, and Jerusalem's al-Aqsa Mosque—Islam's third holiest shrine—floating amid brightly colored plastic crystals.

After another revolution around the plaza, the evening prayer call rang out. I trailed a group of Saudi youths from nearby Yanbu through the Gate of Mercy (one of the oldest entrances to the mosque) to a niche close to the Sacred Chamber within which stands the so-called Perfumed Column. According to histories of the life of Muhammad, this column marks the spot where the Prophet preferred to offer his prayers. Some Muslims believe special blessings are bestowed upon those who pray there today. Before beginning the *tarawih* (a lengthy recitation of Qur'anic verses that occurs every evening during

Ramadan), the imam of the Prophet's Mosque exhorted worshippers to remember the Muslims suffering in Chechnya. Upon leaving the service, I noticed that collection boxes for the Saudi government's Joint Kosovo-Chechnya Relief Committee had been placed outside each of the mosque's exits.

I was treated to a tour of some of Medina's historic sites the following day. My guide, a professor from the city's Islamic University, first drove us to the foothills of Mt. Ohud. There, in 625—the third year of the *hijra* or Islamic calendar that commenced with Muhammad's flight to Medina from Mecca—3,000 Meccan warriors led by the Prophet's own Quraysh tribe confronted a Muslim army of some 1,000 souls. Despite being outnumbered, the Muslims might have won the battle because they were defending from the high ground. Unfortunately, most of the Prophet's 50-odd archers disobeyed orders and withdrew from the battle prematurely, thus allowing the Meccan army to encircle the Muslims. Sixty-four soldiers of Islam were killed and 150, including Muhammad himself, were wounded. The Meccans, believing the Prophet had been killed, withdrew at nightfall, enabling Muhammad—who, after his injury, had been defended by a sword-wielding Medinan woman named Nassibah—and the remnants of his army to escape. Never again would he permit lack of discipline to endanger his forces.

The site of the Battle of Ohud is heavily visited by tourists. A path leading up the small hill the archers had occupied is lined with trinket vendors. The place where Hamza ibn Abd al-Muttalib—Muhammad's paternal uncle who had married only the day before the battle—fell as Islam's first martyr is marked by a small stone just west of a modest-size hill known as al-Rumat. He and several other martyrs are buried in a basketball court–size cemetery surrounded by a whitewashed mud brick wall about 2 meters high atop a plateau near the archers' hill. Despite the Saudis' attempts to discourage the visiting of graves, the cemetery was thronged with Muslims paying their respects.

My guide next took me to the site of the trench dug by the Muslims to defend Medina against a siege by the Meccan army in the fourth year of the *hijra*. Stretching northeast to southwest along the city's unfortified northern flank, the trench was completed in six days by men, including the Prophet, working in round-the-clock shifts. According to historians, it was approximately 3.75 kilometers long, 6.75 meters wide, and 5.25 meters deep. Although no trace of it remains, it is said to have been large enough to dissuade the Meccan cavalry from attempting to cross it, thus neutralizing the Quraysh's most potent weapon. The siege of Medina lasted more than 20 days, during which time some members of the polytheistic tribes confederated with the Quraysh changed sides and one of Medina's Jewish tribes, the Bani Qurayza, turned against its Muslim allies. After the Meccan army withdrew, granting Muhammad a defensive victory that enhanced his status among the many uncommitted Arab tribes, he ordered the execution of all the men of the Bani Qurayza and the enslavement of its women and children.

On Medina's relatively undeveloped southwestern periphery lie the ruins of what my guide said was a "palace" that was home to a prominent Jewish poet named Ka'b bin al-Ashraf who lived during Muhammad's time. Composed of large, finely cut stone blocks forming the outlines of six rooms spread over approximately 250 square meters, the ruins are surrounded by a chain link fence posted with warning signs that state the area is a protected archeological site. It nonetheless appeared to be a convenient place for Medinans to dump their trash. My guide and I stepped gingerly through broken glass and around old pieces of furniture to arrive at the soot-blackened walls. According to my guide, al-Ashraf was among the city's most prominent citizens. He was reputed to have been handsome, with long, black hair, and to have been very popular among the city's females. During the sixth year of the *hijra*, the poet increased his renown by writing verses celebrating, in rather graphic terms, his love of Muslim women.

That same year, Muhammad's army fought a battle against the rebellious Bani Mustaliq tribe, during which his youngest wife, Aisha, was left behind in the city. A Muslim junior officer found her along the way and took her on his camel to the Prophet's campsite, spurring rumors that Aisha had been unfaithful to her husband. Al-Ashraf, according to my guide, set these tales to verse.[6] Following the revelation of the Qur'an's *surah* (chapter) 24 titled "The Light," in which adultery and calumny are condemned, the Prophet ordered the poet's death for slandering Islam. According to my guide, the Muslim volunteer who carried out this first *fatwa* (binding legal decision) lured al-Ashraf out of his palace, grabbed him by his flowing locks, and slashed his throat.

My guide and I offered midday prayers at Quba'a mosque, the first house of worship in the history of Islam. Located in what is now southern Medina, it received its name from the village where the Prophet rested after his flight from Mecca. Muhammad himself is said to have participated in the mosque's construction and to have led prayers there before his home and mosque were built in Medina. According to at least two *hadith* (traditions relating to the words and deeds of the Prophet as recounted by his companions), one who makes his ablutions at home and prays at Quba'a is entitled to a recompense similar to that derived from undertaking an *umra*. Expanded and renovated at the personal expense of King Fahd, the imposing structure with its four, soaring minarets, is a fine example of contemporary Arab architecture, but—unfortunately—little remains to remind visitors of the character of Muhammad's simple, spare testament of faith.

Qiblatayn (meaning two *qiblas*) Mosque also is famous among Medina's plethora of historic houses of worship. Situated atop a narrow ridge in the city's northwestern quarter, it, too, has undergone a recent renovation and expansion underwritten by the Al Saud. Fortunately, it still bears some resemblance to the one-minaret structure wherein the Prophet, halfway through his midday prayers, received the revelation ordering him to change the direction of the *qibla* (direction of prayer) from Jerusalem to Mecca. In full view of his astonished companions, he simply got up, faced the opposite direction, and continued praying. Explanatory texts in Arabic, English, Urdu, and German denote the old *qibla* niche in the mosque today.

About 1.5 kilometers southwest of the Prophet's Mosque in downtown Medina is the station that was the southern terminus of the Hejaz Railway. Built by the Turks in 1908, it occupies a cigar-shaped hectare of prime real estate and is distinguished by its ornate design incorporating traditional Ottoman elements using locally quarried gray stone and imported cream-colored bricks. Abandoned after World War I (during which T.E. Lawrence's Arab army blew up portions of the track to the north), the station still exudes the charm of a simpler, more optimistic era.

The two-story main terminal building is about the size of a small aircraft hanger. Behind it are two single-story outbuildings and a row of dilapidated sheds and workshops. Lined up in the yard opposite the sheds are 34 derelict, narrow-gauge freight and tanker cars along with three rusted-out steam locomotives. According to my guide, a museum was slated to open in the main terminal building several years ago. Some initial renovation work—including replacing most of the building's original slate roof with cheap-looking corrugated fiberglass panels—appeared to have been done, but a look through the windows (the doors all were locked) revealed nothing resembling a museum inside. Across the street in front of the station is what used to be a fancy public garden with a water basin (now buried beneath a major thoroughfare) and the al-Anbariyya Mosque. Built by the Turks as part of the

Medina's Hejaz Railway terminal building, shown from the rear, is similar in design to its sister station in Damascus. (Author)

railway station complex, the mosque's design complements that of the station and, despite what time and progress have done to the city, continues to hint at the Medina that used to be.

The Kiswa (May 2000)

The Kaaba first was covered in the pre-Islamic era following the efforts of the Quraysh, Mecca's most-powerful tribe, to repel repeated raids by the rulers of Yemen. Mecca, having grown rich as the main pilgrimage site on the spice route, was a tempting prize for invaders. The Yemenis' third Hejazi campaign was on the brink of success until its leader, King Tuba'a al-Himyari, contracted a mysterious skin disease. His priests advised him to accede to the Quraysh's demand that he venerate rather than despoil the Kaaba. This he did by following the pilgrim custom of circumambulating it seven times and then shaving his head. The King's condition improved and, to celebrate his recovery, he ordered his soldiers to drape the Kaaba with all the cloth they brought with them on the expedition; legend has it that this first *kiswa* was red. To commemorate their victory over the Yemenis, the then-pagan Quraysh adopted as a religious obligation the practice of covering the Kaaba.

Three narrow-gauge steam locomotives, including this relic, lay in ruins at Medina's Hejaz Railway terminal building. (Author)

The Prophet Muhammad did not render an opinion on the necessity of the *kiswa*. However, he did give the shroud tacit legitimacy in 631, two years after he established Muslim control over Mecca and one year before his death. In that year, the *kiswa* was consumed in a fire started by a Muslim woman who tried to perfume the Kaaba with burning incense, and Muhammad ordered it replaced with a new covering made of striped Yemeni cloth. After his death, the caliphs (successors to the Prophet) established the tradition of regularly covering the Kaaba with new *kiswas* that generally were made of cotton broadcloth imported from Egypt. Caliph Muawiya bin Abu Sufyan is said by Islamic scholars to have draped the Kaaba in silk brocade on the occasion of *Ashura* (the tenth day of the Muslim new year) and then a new cotton shroud at the end of Ramadan. Over the years, the *kiswas* accumulated one on top of the other until it was feared that the Kaaba would collapse under their weight. When the Abbasid Caliph Al-Mahdi performed the hajj in 783, he decreed that only a single cover should adorn the Kaaba, a practice that has continued to this day.

Kiswas were made of various colors, including red and green, until 864, when Caliph Al-Nasir established the tradition of using only black cloth to drape the Kaaba. Following the demise of the Abbasid dynasty and the rise of the Fatimids (circa 945), Egyptian and Yemeni kings alternated years in which they provided new *kiswas*. These were delivered to the elders of the Bani Shayba tribe, whom the Quraysh made keepers of the Kaaba by entrusting them with its key.[7] In 1379, the Egyptian King Al-Salih Ismael established an endowment that provided for a new black *kiswa* for the Kaaba once every five years. This endowment continued until the beginning of the nineteenth century, when the Ottoman sultans in Istanbul assumed responsibility for Mecca and Medina.

After conquering the Hejaz in 1925, Ibn Saud established the following year a factory for producing the *kiswa* in Mecca. Silk, instead of cotton, was now the material of choice because of its durability and prestige: The Al Saud were determined to show the world that they would spare no expense in exercising the custodianship of the two holy places. The downtown factory was demolished in the course of the gargantuan Grand Mosque expansion project in 1971.

The current *kiswa* factory, which occupies a sprawling, spotless compound in a quiet residential district west of the city center (but still in the Muslims-only *haram* zone), was dedicated by King Faysal in 1972. It is next door to the new *Haramayn* (two holy places) Museum, which features artifacts and photos from the expansions of the Grand Mosque and the Prophet's Mosque. The factory employs 76 male workers, all of whom are Saudis. Its administrators boast that their production processes seamlessly merge traditional craftsmanship with modern advances in textile production.

The *kiswa* is made from Italian raw silk. The silk arrives at the factory in skeins of nine-ply thread weighing about 100 grams apiece. Each skein contains approximately 3,000 meters of thread. Once the thread is dyed and tested (the factory has a fully equipped laboratory where threads and cloth are tested for resistance to sun, sweat, weight, fire, and friction), it is woven into 15 pieces measuring 101 centimeter wide by 14 meters long. The fabric is embossed with the following phrases: "O God, there is no god but God and Muhammad is His Messenger"; "the Most Loving, the Beneficent"; "glory be to God and praise be to God"; and "glory to God the Great."

Fitted around the top third of the Kaaba is a 16-piece belt, each segment of which is 95 centimeters wide and 45 centimeters long. It, like the rest of the *kiswa*, is embroidered in silver and gold-covered silver threads with Qur'anic verses in the al-Thuluth style of Arabic calligraphy. Beneath the belt at each corner of the Kaaba, *surah* 112 ("Al-Ikhlas," purity of faith) of the Qur'an is embroidered inside a frame.

Also under the belt, at the same height, are six other Qur'anic verses embroidered in frames, each of which is separated by a lamp-like design in which one of several phrases is written: "O You are the Alive and the Self-Subsisting"; "the Most Gracious, the Most Merciful"; and "praise be to God." A heavily embroidered curtain is hung on the side of the Kaaba where the al-Multazam door is located. It consists of five pieces, the combined area of which is 20.86 square meters. It features the opening *surah* of the Qur'an ("Al-Fatiha") and other verses.

At the beginning of the hajj month (Dhu al-Hijjah), a celebration is held at the factory during which the new but unassembled *kiswa* is presented by the General Director for the Affairs of the Holy Mosque in Mecca and the Prophet's Mosque in Medina to the senior representative of the Bani Shayba tribe, long the guardians of the shrine. Along with the *kiswa*, the elder is presented with an embroidered bag in which the Kaaba key is to be kept. The new *kiswa* replaces the old one of the ninth day of *Dhu al-Hijjah*, also known as the Day of Standing, during which pilgrims are required to spend the day in supplication on the plain of Arafat east of Mecca. The *kiswa* is sewn together on site, lined with a white cotton cloth, and hung one side at a time by ropes suspended from hooks on the Kaaba's roof. The belt and door curtain are added last, the latter being directly mounted to the Kaaba because of its weight.

The *kiswa* factory's managing director took pride in telling me that all his employees are Saudis. This was not the case as recently as five years ago, but the factory has succeeded in training Saudis to perform the meticulous embroidery work that for years was carried out by Afghan and Pakistani expatriate workers. The factory operates an apprenticeship program that trains young Saudis to operate the various automated processes, including two large, Belgian-made jacquard machines. Silk dyeing, calligraphy design, and embroidery all are highly specialized—and prestigious—skills that are performed only by longtime employees who have worked their way up from the factory floor. Top Saudi university scientists compete for yearlong sabbaticals enabling them to staff the testing laboratory. Competition for places in the apprenticeship program and for all manner of jobs, even machine maintenance and janitorial work, is fierce, and each year hundreds of would-be Saudi tea boys are turned away. Although wages are comparable to those of factory jobs elsewhere in the Hejaz, Saudis are highly motivated to play a part in this "labor of love that is pleasing in the eyes of God," according to the managing director.

A public affairs officer in the managing director's office told me that the factory averages 3,000 visitors per year. Many of these are foreign dignitaries who come for a peek at the new *kiswa* before hajj begins. Such dignitaries, the public affairs officer noted, usually are presented with *ihram* garments (requisite male pilgrim attire consisting of two lengths of seamless white cloth akin to towels) that are woven at the factory. These have become highly sought-after souvenirs, he confided, because they bear labels identifying where they were produced. In addition to the *kiswa* and *ihram* garments, the factory makes high-quality Saudi flags for government installations. It also is responsible for the production of manually woven and embellished green silk cloth that is used to drape the Sacred Chamber inside the Prophet's Mosque and to adorn the interior walls of the Kaaba.

The King's Highway (January 2002)

The King's Highway, a hajj route known in the Hejaz as the Darb al-Tabukiyyah, links Damascus with Mecca via Medina, Islam's second-holiest city. Established atop a much older road that was an important corridor for the incense and spice trades during late antiquity, the route allegedly derives its name from the fact that the commodities it carried were bought and sold for princely—nay, kingly—sums. Rome's acceptance of Christianity, and the concomitant decline in cremation ceremonies, dealt a severe blow to the South Arabian incense industry. At around the same time, maritime advances made transporting spices from South Asia cheaper and safer by sea than by land. By 570, the year of the Prophet Muhammad's birth, the traditional overland paths were used only by itinerant merchants and the pilgrims who continued to gather annually in Mecca to worship the tribal idols of their ancestors collected at the Kaaba.[8]

Muhammad appeared at a critical time. Many Hejazis were pagans, but a substantial number practiced Judaism or Christianity. Sectarianism flourished in the Arabian Peninsula, which had become a commercial and cultural backwater, aggravating tribal violence. The Prophet instituted sweeping reforms propelled by faith and, in the process, spawned an empire. Grafting the new onto the old, he required Muslims to make the pilgrimage to Mecca and revived the traditional trade routes to get them there.

Formalization of the King's Highway as a hajj route occurred during the Umayyad period (661–750) when the caliphate was located in Damascus. Caliph Omar bin Abd al-Aziz (who ruled from 717–720) is credited with establishing the first of what became a string of stone caravansaries, called *qal'ats* (castles) by locals, where pilgrim camel

trains could find water, shelter, and protection from marauding tribesmen. Generally spaced a week's ride apart, the qal'ats were maintained
by successive Islamic dynasties. In all, more than 30 of these medieval
motels stretched from Damascus to Mecca.

In one of the events precipitating the Third Crusade, Reginald of
Chatillon, the Islamophobic prince of Kerak (the ancient citadel of the
Moabites near the Dead Sea in what is now western Jordan), hatched
a scheme to defile Mecca and Medina and destroy the Kaaba. During
1182–83, he built a fleet of ships and sailed down the Red Sea, raiding
and terrorizing coastal towns in Egypt and Arabia. He and his forces
marched inland from near present-day Aqaba and down the King's
highway toward Medina, plundering all the way. They were met and
defeated just outside the city by tribesmen under the command of al-
Malik al-Adil, brother of Saladin (Salah al-Din Yusuf ibn Ayyub), the
Sultan of Egypt and Syria (who ruled from 1175–93). Prince Reginald
escaped, but many of his men were not so fortunate. Captured by al-
Malik al-Adil, they were taken to Egypt and beheaded.

During the Ottoman period (which began in the sixteenth century),
the Turks built garrisons in proximity to some of the qal'ats and rein-
forced others as fortresses. In 1908, the Turks inaugurated the Hejaz
Railway, more properly known as the Chemin de Fer du Hedjaz or CFH
(the initials were painted on the sides of the rolling stock by its French-
speaking Damascene maintenance personnel). Billed by Sultan Abd al-
Hamid II as a religious endeavor and funded through salary tithes,
postage stamps, and the sale of sheepskins culled from animals sacrificed at the conclusion of the hajj, the railway was in fact intended as a
way to move troops quickly into the Hejaz in case of rebellion.
Establishing 41 stations from Medina to the border with Jordan alone,
CFH engineers sited some stations at or near the King's Highway qal'ats.

The result was that the time it took to traverse the 1,302 kilometers
from Damascus to Medina was cut from two months to three days and
three nights (at a maximum speed of 60 miles per hour). Following the
end of the Ottoman Empire at the close of the Great War, the CFH
was operated by the Hashemites until 1924, when Ibn Saud had nearly
completed his conquest of the Hejaz. Riyadh undertook several still-
born attempts to revive the railway in the 1960s and 1970s. Although
a new plan to rebuild it was announced in late 2001, the existence of a
more-than-adequate modern freeway linking Medina to points north
suggests that such a project would not be economically viable.

I traveled a portion of the King's Highway during the course of a visit
to Medina. The first stop was the CFH terminal, a beautiful old structure

(similar to its sister station in downtown Damascus) located in the *haram* area about 1.5 kilometers southwest of the Prophet's Mosque. The hectare-size plot it occupies is said to previously have featured a caravansary surrounded by a date-palm plantation owned by Ottoman pashas; proceeds from the sale of the dates were used to fund the hajj journeys of indigent Syrian pilgrims. The site currently is undergoing commercial development. The terminal itself will be converted into a shopping center, while the remaining outbuildings and rusting CFH locomotives and rolling stock appear destined for oblivion.

Proceeding north from Medina, the King's Highway stretches west of the current road leading to Tabuk. After approximately 20 kilometers, a surprisingly well-maintained dirt track winds behind a mosque and across the grassy Wadi al-Hamd. From there, an 83-kilometer excursion (one way) on tarmac, atop portions of the old CFH railbed, and along dry river bottoms, revealed the following three "castles":

—*Qal'at Hafirah* lies just 700 meters west of the Tabuk road on the edge of a swampy palm grove. Measuring approximately 210 square meters and some 6 meters high, it is constructed of black lava stone and features Ottoman-era battlements as well as a 2-meter-tall parapet. The courtyard contains older, Umayyad-era walls and a working well.

—Thirty-seven kilometers further north, on the south bank of the Wadi Rashad, lie the ruins of *Qal'at Abyar Naseef*. Situated amid cultivated fields, the 2-meter-high walls consist of locally quarried red, green, and brown stone blocks, giving what is left of the building a friendly, even cheerful aspect. It measures about 17 by 20 meters and can be difficult to find without help from local farmers.

—*Qal'at Shajwa* is located another 45 kilometers north and 6 kilometers east of the CFH railbed amid a palm garden in Wadi Khaybar. Unlike the others, it retains some of its original, cream-colored plaster coating. Measuring nearly 250 square meters, it is a two-story, blockhouse-style building similar to Dhat al-Hajj, the northernmost *qal'at* (in Tabuk) before the border in Jordan. Nearby is an 11 by 5 meter rectangular *birqat* (masonry pool). It was a fifth full of rainwater and infested with mosquito larvae when I visited.

I also traveled to several of the *qal'ats* on the King's Highway route south from Medina to Mecca. Each had been fortified by the Ottoman Turks in the nineteenth century. These included the following:

—*Hisn (fort) Juhfah*, located 9 kilometers southeast of Rabigh in Wadi al-Halq. A massive, lava-stone structure missing its northern wall, it

Qal'at Hafirah, one of the better-preserved caravansaries along the King's Highway, was built using dark lava stone found in abundance in the Hejaz. (Author)

stands alone amid the rolling dunes of the coastal plain. It sports 11 high arches supporting a watchman's gallery on the southern wall and a nearby well fed by an underground stream. This *qal'at* served as a *miqaat* or ritual ablution point for pilgrims until a modern facility was built nearby in 1970.

Hisn Juhfah, a *qal'at* that formerly served as an ablution point for pilgrims, remains a formidable presence on the coastal plain near Rabigh. (Author)

—*Qal'at Khulays*, a well-preserved redoubt situated atop a 50-meter-high pile of basalt boulders. Water was provided by a dam located on a stream that once ran through Wadi Marwani, approximately 2 kilometers south of the *qal'at*. The valley's water supply has, since the mid-1960s, been diverted to Jeddah, and wells in this once-prime agricultural area now are deeper than 40 meters and increasingly saline. Notable features of this *qal'at* include the still-visible clearings pilgrims made for their tents amid the rocks surrounding the building, as well as the plethora of stone hand tools lying about.

—*Qal'at Usfan* lies 50 kilometers south of Khulays in the middle of a freeway interchange northeast of Jeddah. Although its volcanic blocks have been "mined" and vandalized by locals, it still resembles a smaller version of Hisn Juhfah, with arched walls. It sits atop a small granite outcropping and has a vaulted cellar that presumably was used by the Turks to store ammunition or water brought by donkeys from nearby Wadi Faydah.

—*Qal'at Dukhan*, the last King's Highway caravansary before Mecca, is located among lush fields at the base of the Harrat Rahat lava plateau between Jamoum and Hadat al-Sham. But for the absence of a cellar, it is identical to Qal'at Usfan, albeit much better preserved.

Qal'at Usfan, a familiar sight northeast of Jeddah, features a vaulted cellar. (Author)

Ample fresh water delivered by a still-functioning Umayyad-era *qanat* (underground canal) system fills two *birqats*—one of which is circular and nearly 100 meters in diameter—that are less than 1 kilometer away.[9]

It is easy to forget in this age of convenience how difficult life in Arabia was before the introduction of motor vehicles, electricity, and air conditioning. The sometimes less-than-welcoming Hejazi culture was forged on the anvil of merciless heat and humidity, with the search for water, shade, and bread daily obsessions. Recognizing that the inhabitants were simultaneously dependent on and hostile to foreigners, perspicacious overlords established the King's Highway to facilitate the procession of pilgrims into the holy land, while at the same time protecting them from local predation. As romantic ruins, the *qal'ats* hearken back to a bygone era of hardship yet stand as peculiarly apt metaphors for the ambivalence with which Hejazis regard the foreigners in their midst today.

The Darb Zubaydah (January 2002)

Although parts of the Darb Zubaydah had been in use during the pre-Islamic era, a road for Mesopotamians going to Mecca formally was established by the Abbasid caliphs, in particular Harun al-Rashid (who ruled from 786–809) of "Arabian Nights" fame. His favorite wife, Zubaydah, took a keen interest in the welfare of pilgrims and provided much of the funding for the construction of the numerous *birqats*, or freshwater pools, and associated caravansaries that define the trail. They were set at distances no more than a pilgrim could traverse in a day, usually 12 to 30 kilometers, depending on the terrain. The pools were ingeniously engineered to take advantage of underwater aquifers or rainwater runoff to fill them. In some areas, extensive networks of *qanats* or underground canals were installed to provide the pools with water drained from nearby valleys.

Heading south by southwest from Kufa, the Darb Zubaydah enters present-day Saudi Arabia near Rafha and then traverses the Wadi Zubalah past Shamat al-Akbad. Proceeding south through al-Ajfar, it meets Shayb Abu al-Kurush, where it cuts west to avoid Qassim, the residents of which were regarded as fanatical primitives by the Abbasids. The Darb skirts Ha'il before proceeding south again through al-Rawdah and Sumayrah. It tracks along the Jabal Mawan and down Wadi al-Amira before reaching Mahad al-Dhahab, the site of ancient diggings reputed to be the fabled mines of King Solomon (commercial quantities of gold are extracted there to this day). The pilgrim trail then meanders southwest through several isolated valleys as it approaches Ta'if and Mecca.

The Darb Zubaydah also was known as the Darb al-Sharqi (eastern road) to distinguish it from the King's Highway, the older Syrian hajj route leading south from Damascus. British adventurer Sir Richard Burton, disguised as an Anglo-Indian named Abdallah, joined a pilgrim caravan heading east from Medina in 1853 and thence down the Darb to Mecca. In a subsequent book about his hajj experience, Burton wrote that he and his group were set upon in the barren Wadi al-Mahalik (literally, Perilous Valley) by Utaybi tribesmen before arriving at the green, vastly more pleasant Wadi al-Laymoun (Lime Valley), where they rested before entering the holy city. Wadi al-Mahalik denotes what today is known as the southern portion of Wadi al-Aqiq , some 75 kilometers northeast of Ta'if. Two pools, Birqats al-Khurabah and al-Aqiq, are located on the Darb Zubaydah 20 and 36 kilometers, respectively, north of where the caravan was attacked. Wadi al-Laymoun is identified with the vale encompassing al-Madiq, the final Darb Zubaydah *birqat*, located some 30 kilometers northeast of Mecca. Burton's caravan stopped at all three.[10]

In the course of a trip to the Ta'if-Mecca area, I followed a portion of the Darb Zubaydah and examined the three pools Burton visited. Birqat al-Aqiq lies about 400 meters to the west of the Ashayrah-Mohani road on the eastern edge of Wadi al-Aqiq. Partially restored by the Saudi government in 1973, it is distinguishable on the horizon from the bleak, rock-strewn high desert by the stands of sizable cypress and acacia trees that have grown up around it. Recent rains had completely filled the 5-meter-deep, pumice-block pool via a channel running into its southwest corner. Measuring some 49 meters on each side, the walled *birqat* has six openings allowing access to the water.

Several ruined shelters and the possible remains of a fortress mark the eastern approach to the pool. To the north is a modern, concrete cistern measuring 60 square meters that serves the needs of several nearby villages. On the western side, perched at the edge of the *wadi* (dry river valley), resides a family of goatherds. In response to my questions, the wizened head of the household said his long-deceased uncle was assigned to protect the *birqat* after its restoration. Neighbors, he explained, wanted to demolish the old pool because a number of children and animals have drowned in it through the years, prompting fears that the site is inhabited by *jinns* or evil spirits.

Birqat al-Khurabah is about 16 kilometers southeast of the al-Aqiq pool near the hamlet of al-Adil. It, too, was restored in 1973. It is reached by driving off-road along a 12-kilometers-long, 2-meter-wide, 1-meter-high mound indicating the presence of a *qanat*. Reputed to be the most impressive of all the *birqats*, its elaborateness is explained by the fact that it once served as a *miqaat* (prescribed ablution point) for pilgrims. Al-Khurabah is composed of two pools, both of which were full to the brim during my visit, connected by two tunnels. The western *birqat*, into which the *qanat* empties, is rectangular, measuring some 36 by 28 meters, with stepped sides. The eastern pool is circular in design, with a diameter of about 14 meters. As at al-Aqiq, both are enclosed by a 1-meter-high, volcanic-block wall punctuated at regular intervals by water-access openings.

On top of the tunnels and built of the same volcanic stone is a small, twin-domed structure once used by pilgrims to perform the purification rituals and don their *ihram* or hajj garments. A new, concrete cistern (identical to the one at al-Aqiq) lies just to the east. A tanker truck from al-Faysaliyyah, a suburb of Ashayrah, was being filled there when I visited. Questioned about the site, the Yemen-born driver replied that al-Khurabah's water is prized for its sweet taste and medicinal qualities. During the exchange that followed, the driver grinned broadly when I mentioned the story about *jinns* at al-Aqiq. He described the locals as fond of inventing such tales to frighten away visitors, stating "they wish to keep their waters to themselves."

Just over 40 kilometers south of Birqat al-Khurabah, and 1.5 kilometers west of the camel racecourse by the Ashayrah exit off the Riyadh

The Saudi Government restored Birqat al-Khurabah, the most elaborate of the pools along the Darb Zubaydah, in 1973. (Author)

highway, lie the remains of the Okaz *souk* (market). Okaz was the largest and best-known of the pre-Islamic market towns that served as forums to share news, resolve tribal disputes, deliver sermons (by religious authorities, including, in this case, the Archbishop of Najran), and recite *qasidas* or odes (the traditional form or Arab entertainment). Many of these odes celebrated great deeds and men of bygone days. According to Hejazi legend, a poet named Imru al-Qays won renown for composing many fine *qasidas*. One of his best works, along with the work of six other poets, was memorialized by being written in gold thread on black cloth and hung on the exterior of the Kaaba at Mecca, a practice that may have helped to inspire the custom of draping the sacred building in an embroidered cloak called the *kiswa*.

The ruins of Birqat al-Madiq are found near the village of al-Hazm, some 500 meters north of the Jeddah exit of the aptly named Ta'if truck road at the mouth of the small, steep-sided Wadi al-Laymoun. The 15 by 20 meter, aboveground pool sits on a small bluff set against the vivid green backdrop of palm, papaya, and—yes—lime trees. Its 3-meter-high walls, three of which remain standing, are made of beige stone blocks. A well-trimmed staircase still leads into the pool on the northern side. To the south, one can see the remains of an aqueduct and numerous water channels carved into the adjacent canyon wall.

The ruins of the Okaz market, which served as a forum for sharing news in the pre-Islamic era, suggest it featured a vaulted roof. (Author)

The last of the Darb Zubaydah pools, and thus the closest to Mecca, al-Madiq nevertheless ranks among the most obscure. Deprived of easy access by the embankments of the nearby freeway, and challenging to find even if you know where to look, the *birqat* and its surroundings retain much of the unspoiled charm one imagines they boasted of in Burton's day. The untouched grasses and shrubs carpeting the canyon floor suggest that even local herdsmen and their ravenous flocks find Wadi al-Laymoun inaccessible.

The Darb Zubaydah was a remarkable and enduring success. It conquered the barriers of distance, climate, and terrain to link Mecca, Islam's birthplace, with the palaces and parvenus of a new empire extending far beyond the Arabian Peninsula. Its *birqats* stand as a testament not only to the vision of its creators and the skill of its engineers, but also to the determination of millions of pilgrims who, like Burton, braved the elements and the locals to perform the hajj.

The Mawaqeet (December 2001—March 2002)

The hajj is as much a legal as it is a spiritual affair. A host of rules stipulate the proper comportment of pilgrims, including the intent they must have when approaching Mecca. Ritual purification or *ihram* is the physical manifestation of lawful intent.

Ritual purification begins with personal cleanliness. Following ablutions, pilgrims dress in special garments and offer specific prayers. As Islam evolved during the Prophet's lifetime and in the decades following his death, five points—each known as a *miqaat*, collectively known as the *mawaqeet*—were identified as the places at which pilgrims should assume *ihram* before entering into the proximity of the holy city. All were sited along the traditional hajj routes. Looked at from above, the exclusive zone defined by imaginary lines connecting the *mawaqeet* (and Jeddah, unofficially recognized as the sixth or "western" *miqaat*) form an irregular teardrop shape dripping north to south in the Hejaz.

The northernmost *miqaat*, as well as the furthest (330 kilometers) from Mecca, is Abyar Ali. Also known as Dhu al-Hulayfah, it is the largest and most attractive of the five. Located 9 kilometers southwest of the Prophet's Mosque, it serves as the ablution point for the residents of Medina and those passing through Islam's second-holiest city. The cream-and-white, vaguely Andalusian-style stucco facility is plainly visible near the non-Muslim exit off the Mecca-Medina highway. According to a plaque on the wall of the imposing prayer hall, the *miqaat* was "expanded" in 1992; in fact, it is a completely new facility that entirely swallowed its far-more-modest predecessor.

Abyar Ali, the northernmost *miqaat*, is just south of the Medina city limits and sports a ziggurat-style minaret. (Author)

Abyar Ali features separate, warehouse-size shower and changing rooms for men and women, a soaring, ziggurat-style minaret, and a capacious parking lot. Water is drawn from the "wells of Ali" beneath the complex (and for which it is named). On the day of my visit in early January 2002, the *miqaat* was vacant, much to the disappointment of the dozen or so vendors of *ihram* garments, hajj belts (money belts used by men to secure their valuables and their lower towels), sandals, and other pilgrimage accouterments, ensconced in little Hajj Ministry–approved kiosks studding the site.

I stopped by al-Juhfah, the second most-northern *miqaat*, in late December 2001. Serving as the ablution point for the residents of Syria and Egypt as well as pilgrims passing through those lands, it is located east of the town of Rabigh, about 150 kilometers north of Mecca. The original *miqaat* was at *Hisn* (fort) Juhfah on the King's Highway from Damascus in Wadi al-Halq. In 1972, the Saudi government built a new facility several kilometers to the southeast atop the well that used to service the fort. Despite its large parking area, the whitewashed, institutional-looking *miqaat* (featuring a skeletal minaret that could pass for a water tower) is relatively small and gives the impression of being rarely used. A Hejazi friend subsequently informed me that although

Al-Juhfah is the least attractive of the five *miqaat* and is infrequently used. (Author)

buses carrying foreign pilgrims invariably stop at the *miqaat*, Saudis traveling by car from south of Medina generally assume *ihram* either in their homes or in Rabigh proper, rather than detour off the highway along some 10 kilometers of dirt track to the official ablution point.

I traveled to Dhat 'Irq, the ablution point for the people of Iraq, Khurasan (eastern Iran/western Afghanistan), and central and northern Najd, and those passing through those areas, when I examined the Darb Zubaydah in mid-January 2002. The original *miqaat*, located at Birqat al-Khurabah (see photo on page 39), was the third most-northern ablution point until 1995, when it was moved to its present location approximately 16 kilometers northwest of Ta'if near the escarpment road and the al-Hada Sheraton hotel. The new *miqaat*, called Wadi Muhrim, is now the second most-southern of the five. It is about the same size and design as the al-Juhfah structure, only more nicely rendered, with light brown "Riyadh stone" cladding that is trimmed with white marble and a low-rise minaret graced with a black marble balcony. Perched on a small promontory, it has a commanding view of the valley below and a gigantic satellite receiver dish in the center of its rather cramped parking lot. Several carloads of Kingdom-resident Filipino *umra* pilgrims were present when I arrived, and an adjacent row of small shops proffering the usual paraphernalia appeared to be doing a reasonably brisk business.

The Wadi Muhrim miqaat sits atop a promontory overlooking the escarpment road, which winds down to Jeddah and the Red Sea. (Author)

The present *miqaat* at al-Sayy al-Kabir was established on the grounds of a facility that burned to the ground in 1975. Also called Qarn al-Manazil ("village of many residences")—owing to the large number of homes that once surrounded it, shared the ample water from the well beneath the structure, and probably perished in the same conflagration—it is the ablution point for the people of southern Najd and Ta'if, and people passing through those regions. Located on the truck road about 35 kilometers north of Ta'if and 60 kilometers east-by-northeast of Mecca, al-Sayy al-Kabir is now the third most-northern *miqaat*. Spare and unadorned like al-Juhfah, it is about half again as large and lies in a shallow, easily accessed valley just north of the highway. Its large parking lot has no vendor kiosks. During my visit, however, signs were posted inviting pilgrims to peruse the wares available at several nearby truck stops.

Yalamlam, also known as Al-Sa'adiyyah, is the *miqaat* of the people of Yemen and neighboring countries, and those passing through these areas. The southernmost ablution point, it is on the eastern side of the Jeddah-Jizan Highway before the town of al-Layth, about 125 kilometers south of Mecca. It has a mid-size parking lot but is the second

The al-Sayy al-Kabir *miqaat*, located along the truck road from Jeddah to Ta'if, was established on the grounds of a previous facility that burned to the ground in 1975. (Author)

largest of the *mawaqeet*. Its two towering black-and-white minarets dominate the red-roofed, gray marble edifice and can be seen for miles around on the *tihama*, the fetid, featureless coastal plain south of Jeddah. Despite being the first *miqaat* I visited, and therefore the earliest in terms of hajj preparations, it also was the busiest: Several busloads of visitors as well as a convoy of trucks pulled into the facility when I was there on December 26, 2001. One of the bus drivers told me he was transporting *umra* pilgrims from the southern Asir Governorate. The original Yalamlam is located 45 kilometers to the north in a valley bearing the same name. Unfortunately, entry to the area had been impossible since mid-December because of flooding. Poor roads and a frequent surfeit of unwanted water probably prompted the establishment of the new ablution point in 1979.

As the gateways to the hajj, the *mawaqeet* hold a profound spiritual significance for Muslims. They are icons of the Hejaz, but they always have been more important to visitors from elsewhere. Many pilgrims today travel by air and assume *ihram* as their planes enter the teardrop-shaped exclusive zone outline by the ablution points; Saudi Arabian

The twin minarets of the Yalamlam *miqaat* can be seen for miles around on the flat coastal plain. (Author)

Airlines helpfully informs passengers when to do so. Although Muhammad allowed those living within the *mawaqeet* to undertake ritual purification in their residences, Hejazis from outside this zone tend to follow the same practice and rarely, if ever, stop at a *miqaat* on the road to Mecca.

CHAPTER 3
The Hajj

Religion points to that area of human experience
where in one way or another man comes upon
mystery as a summons to pilgrimage.
                    —Frederick Buechner

To fly into Jeddah at any time, but particularly around the hajj, is to witness the bizarre sight of heretofore normally attired Muslim men rushing to the bathrooms and emerging dressed in what appear to be sheets or towels.[1] With one length of white, seamless cloth wrapped around his waist and another draped across one or both shoulders, the flip-flop clad would-be pilgrim appears less like a penitent than an *Animal House* extra who somehow got lost on the way to the toga party scene. But with the anxiety of one about to meet his maker etched upon his face, it is clear that this soul is not in town to party—at least not yet. For visitors to Saudi Arabia wishing to perform the hajj or the *umra* (the off-season or "minor" pilgrimage that encompasses some of the hajj rituals), the arrival at King Abd al-Aziz International Airport, with its buzzing fluorescent bulbs, overflowing Turkish toilets, and sadistic customs officials, is merely the beginning of a series of obstacles—sacred and profane—that will test the mettle of his or her faith in ways it never before has been tested.

The most daunting problem facing most pilgrims is simply figuring out where to go and what to do at what time. Despite the hajj having occurred every year for more than 14 centuries, there is no authoritative

guidebook informing visitors about how the pilgrimage is to be conducted. The reason for this lack of information is simple: The Saudi
government, in order to accommodate ever-growing numbers of
Muslims seeking to fulfill their obligation to uphold one of the five pillars of the faith, has had to bend what die-hard traditionalists regard
as immutable rules concerning the performance of the various rites.
For an event equivalent in size to 10 simultaneous Super Bowls, the
hajj is nothing if not an enormous logistics challenge, one that generations of officials in the Kingdom have spent their entire professional
lives orchestrating. For them, a successful pilgrimage, one unmarred
by natural or man-made disasters, can mean promotions and expres-
sions of royal gratitude (not infrequently in the form of cars, jobs for
relatives, and the like). A bad hajj puts their careers, and their families'
prospects, in jeopardy. Small wonder, then, that—in this behemoth of
a spiritual event—religious considerations generally take a back seat to
more earthly concerns.

The hajj fascinated me like nothing else during my time in Saudi
Arabia. I knew I had to undertake it if for no other reason than to
maintain my bona fides as a professed Muslim. But I also felt drawn to
the experience, much as I imagine photo-journalists and reporters are
drawn to war zones and other life-threatening scenes. I wanted to go
on the pilgrimage so that I could report knowledgeably and humanely
about an event so central to the lives of Muslims in general and
Hejazis in particular. I strove mightily to grasp the appeal of something that, at first (and, in my case, second) glance appears eminently
unappealing—a glorified Islamic campout with 2 million strangers.

Like most other would-be pilgrims, I lacked fundamental knowledge
about what the hajj, in actuality, entails. Because Hejazis, especially
Jeddawis, are known for making Mecca a second home, with some
embarking on the pilgrimage year after year, I was able to learn much
from well-informed locals. Several of these locals were employed by
Jeddah-based Islamic nongovernmental organizations and government-
financed *da'wa* (Islamic proselytizing) outfits that helped me to flesh
out my bare-bones understanding of the rituals and their significance.
Another contact working at the Hajj Ministry provided me with details
concerning how Saudi officialdom wished the pilgrimage to be performed. All were able to trace for me how the hajj has changed over
time, what rules have been cast aside or revised, and the successes—
and failures—the Al Saud have experienced since it began administer-
ing the pilgrimage in 1925. This context was of enormous help as I
began drafting in early 2000 an unclassified hajj guide for U.S.-origin

pilgrims coming to the holy cities. No other single report of mine met with as much immediate and positive feedback from Washington. I revised and reissued the cable before the pilgrimages of 2001 and 2002.

In addition to examining the hajj from the visitors' point of view, I wanted to convey a sense of what Saudi officials saw themselves up against each year as the pilgrimage drew near. The second report in this chapter examines some of the preparations undertaken by the Saudis in the run-up to the hajj of 2002. What I learned is that preparations for the next pilgrimage begin even before the current one ends, with the government—particularly the Hajj and Interior Ministries—consumed by the event for significant portions of the year. It is perhaps helpful to view the roles these two ministries play as constituting the alpha and the omega of a conflicted official theology that both loves and loathes foreigners. The Hajj Ministry does all within its considerable budgetary power to provide for a reasonably comfortable, safe, and satisfying pilgrimage experience. It facilitates the invitations, visas, flights, transport, accommodations, and care and feeding of "God's guests." In sum, it handles pilgrims from their points of origin to their arrival, settles them into an established infrastructure, and moves on to plan for the next year. The Interior Ministry picks up where the Hajj Ministry leaves off. It keeps tabs on visitors, makes sure they stay out of trouble, punishes them if they do not, and attempts to see to it that they leave when the pilgrimage is over.

During my time in the Hejaz, Interior Minister Nayif bin Abd al-Aziz—citing concerns about the proclivity of hajj visitors to overstay their visas and attempt to work illegally in Saudi Arabia—staged each year a series of highly publicized roundups aimed at demonstrating that Mecca and Jeddah in particular were plagued by criminal gangs composed of pilgrimage overstayers. Because the Minister also controls the Saudi media, these dragnets (and the accompanying slice-of-life vignettes illustrating the danger to well-meaning citizens in providing alms to seemingly innocent disabled and child beggars) were extraordinarily well publicized.

The success of this media blitz enabled the Interior Minister to blunt a Hajj Ministry plan—one supported, not surprisingly, by the Kingdom's chambers of commerce—that called for permitting pilgrims to travel for one month throughout the Kingdom, not just to the holy cities and Jeddah, while visiting for the hajj or *umra*. Although Hajj Minister Iyad Madani (a nonroyal) eventually did gain greater latitude for foreigners during their visits, Prince Nayif won approval for a measure forcing all visitors to register and seek admission to the

Kingdom through authorized pilgrimage travel and service providers. These, in turn, were to be held responsible for making sure everyone who entered left when they were supposed to. The fee the predominately Saudi tour companies had to pay for each overstayer, initially set at less than $1,000, subsequently was raised to more than $2,500. Moreover, the Interior Ministry has enforced guidelines that result in only older, married, well-off visitors receiving pilgrimage visas allowing travel beyond Jeddah and the holy cities.

Of course, even the Interior Ministry's stringent guidelines cannot prevent the hajj—ostensibly an apolitical event—from being used for nefarious purposes. Saudi Arabian National Guard and police personnel, charged with safeguarding the Kingdom's security, are a soft touch when it comes to admitting Muslims bent on answering God's call to come to Mecca. It is well known, for example, that members of various Islamic terrorist organizations meet in Mecca under the pretext of performing the pilgrimage. Since its revolution in 1979, Iran's government has seeded its hajj delegation with provocateurs whose sole aim is to ensure a noisy "denunciation of the infidels" (that is, anti-United States) protest. Crazies from Qadhafi's Libya, Lebanese militiamen, Palestinian suicide bombers, and Kashmiri "freedom fighters" all have passed through the holy cities seemingly unchanged by the event's ultimate message: All human beings are siblings and we'd do well to make the best of this life and learn to live together.

What I find most remarkable about the hajj, however, is that it has not had more problems. Although the event regularly witnesses devastating fires, stampedes, and accidents of all sorts, the mortality rate among pilgrims is not appreciably higher than that of a comparably sized urban population in the Arabian Peninsula.[2] This is despite the fact that some pilgrims, particularly the aged and infirm, go with the intent of dying in the holy land, believing that by so doing they bypass the long wait in the grave for the Day of Judgment and ascend, like martyrs, straight to heaven. The miracle of the hajj, as I see it, is that it takes place at all. In an age characterized by cynicism and mistrust, the pilgrimage manages to pull together a fairly disparate collection of humans celebrating their common condition. For some, the event reaffirms their belief that we all are bound to worship and give thanks to God the creator. I have known others, however, who came out of the hajj as distinctly more secular beings than when they went in. To a person, they also were moved by the spectacle of a sea of humanity striving together in what approximated harmony, and—if less God-fearing—they emerged with a greater appreciation of the value of each and every one of their fellow human beings, "infidels" included. The third report in this chapter recounts my experiences at the blessedly catastrophe-free hajj of 2002.

Soup to Nuts (1999–2002)

The hajj, Islam's fifth pillar, is required at least once in the lifetime of all Muslims who are physically and financially capable of undertaking it.[3] Its rituals derive from pre-Islamic rites as well as practices introduced by the Prophet Muhammad following the Muslim conquest of Mecca, most notably the example he set during his last pilgrimage in 632, the year of his death.

The hajj takes place in and around Mecca, Islam's holiest city. By way of orientation, Mecca lies in a hot, dry valley 65 kilometers east of Jeddah, the main port of entry for pilgrims arriving from abroad. If one draws a line east-by-southeast from the Kaaba (the black-draped, cube-shaped, stone-block building at the center of the Grand Mosque and the focal point of Muslim worship) to Jabal al-Rahmah (the Mountain of Mercy, at which the climax of the pilgrimage takes place), the first 4 kilometers along the line would be Mecca. The next 4 kilometers would be Mina, site of the main pilgrim encampment. The following 3.25 kilometers would be Muzdalifah (the location of another encampment), and the final 7 kilometers would be the plain of Arafat, where Jabal al-Rahmah is located. Medina, home of the Prophet's Mosque and tomb, is approximately 340 kilometers north of Mecca. Although pilgrims are not required to visit Islam's second-holiest city, many—particularly those coming from abroad—do.

According to a *hadith* (a verified narrative describing the words of or example set by Muhammad), the Prophet was asked by a follower "what is the most praiseworthy of deeds?" Muhammad replied, "Believing in the oneness of God and in his Messenger." Asked what came next, the Prophet responded "fighting in the cause of God." Pushed to identify the next most-praiseworthy deed, he said "a sin-free hajj."

Another *hadith* states that the Prophet told his followers that "he who performs hajj without violating it with sexual activity or an act of disobedience will return home as sin-free as the day he was born." He went on to enumerate preconditions to undertaking the pilgrimage:

—Islam (submission before God),
—Adulthood,
—Sanity,

—Freedom,

—Capability, and

—A *mahram* (related male escort) if one is female.

Four *arkaan*, or indispensable rites, are incumbent upon all pilgrims. Missing any of them renders one's hajj null and void:

—*Ihram* (assuming a state of ritual purity),

—Presence at Arafat on the ninth day of the pilgrimage month (the Day of Standing),

—Obligatory *tawwaf* (seven circumambulations of the Kaaba), and

—The *sayy* (seven one-way trips between the hillocks of al-Safa and al-Marwa that are incorporated into the Grand Mosque).

In addition, there are five *wajibaat* or duties that must be undertaken by all pilgrims, the omission of which requires 10 days of fasting (three in Mecca and seven once the pilgrims returns home) or a *hadi* (sacrificial animal) to be killed in Mecca and its meat distributed to the poor.[4]

—Entering *ihram* from a *miqaat* (a prescribed point in time and space),

—Staying at Arafat until sunset on the ninth day of the hajj month,

—Spending the following evening in Muzdalifah,

—Spending the nights following the lapidations (stonings) of the *jamaraat* (pillars representing Satan and his temptations) in Mina, and

—Completing a farewell *tawwaf*.

A Muslim is required to make a statement of intent to perform hajj before undertaking the pilgrimage. It need not be expressed aloud; the acts of preparing and departing for hajj are understood as signifying one's intent. Ritual purification or *ihram* is the physical manifestation of this intent. Before entering into *ihram*, one must ensure personal cleanliness. This involves clipping finger- and toenails, trimming mustaches, plucking or shaving off armpit and pubic hair, and performing either *wudhu'* (standard preprayer ablutions) or taking a bath or shower (the preferred option, particularly for menstruating or postnatal women). Men wear two seamless white towel-like garments, one wrapped around the waist (and normally held in place with a cotton duck money belt known locally as a hajj belt) and the other draped over the left shoulder. They may not wear underwear, head covers, socks, gloves, or footwear that covers the heel. Women dress in plain versions of their ordinary clothing and keep their heads covered, but they are not permitted to wear gloves or face veils.

One enters the state of *ihram* at a *miqaat* (the plural is *mawaqeet*), which exist in two dimensions. There is the *miqaat* of time, encompassing the months of the hajj season: Shawwal, Dhu al-Qa'dah, and the first 10 days of Dhu al-Hijjah. Then there is the *miqaat* of space. Muslims intending to perform the pilgrimage must assume *ihram* before crossing the imaginary lines connecting five points in the Hejaz, each of which features a mosque and the following extensive ablution facilities for this purpose:

—Abyar Ali (also known as Dhu al-Hulayfah): The *miqaat* of the residents of Medina and pilgrims passing through the city. Located 9 kilometers southwest of the Prophet's Mosque (and some 330 kilometers north of Mecca), it is the furthest away from the Kaaba.
—Al-Juhfah: The *miqaat* of the residents of Syria and Egypt, as well as pilgrims passing through those states. It is a site near the village of Rabigh, some 150 kilometers north of Mecca.
—Yalamlam (or al-Sa'adiyyah): The *miqaat* of the people of Yemen, neighboring lands, and those traveling through them. It is on the eastern side of the Jeddah-Jizan highway before the village of al-Layth, some 125 kilometers south of Mecca.
—Al-Sayy al-Kabir (also called Qarn al Manazil): The *miqaat* of the people of southern Najd and Ta'if, and pilgrims passing through those areas. It is about 60 kilometers cast-by-northeast of Mecca.
—Dhat 'Irq (or al-Khurabah): The *miqaat* of the people of Iraq, Khurasan, and central and northern Najd, and pilgrims traversing those regions. Originally a stop on the Darb Zubaydah, the old pilgrim trail from Kufa, approximately 130 kilometers northeast of Mecca; the modern *miqaat*, called Wadi Muhrim, is located 16 kilometers northwest of Ta'if.

There are seven things a pilgrim must not do while in *ihram*:

—Trim, pluck, or shave hair from any part of the body;
—Clip finger- or toenails;
—Cover the face if no male strangers are around (female);
—Wear perfume;
—Consummate marriage;
—Have sexual intercourse; and
—Contact a member of the opposite sex skin-to-skin or engage in activities that might lead to such contact, such as kissing or fondling.

A Muslim may stipulate a condition on God when entering into *ihram* in case he or she is unable to complete the hajj. This is done by reciting, "O God! My *ihram* will be terminated whenever you withhold me." When this is done, one does not have to offer an extra *hadi* or return the following year to make up for an incomplete hajj unless this is the pilgrim's first, in which case he or she must return to complete the pilgrimage.

There are three varieties of hajj: *Tamattu', qiraan,* and *ifraad:*

—In the *tamattu'*, the pilgrim enters *ihram* with the intention of performing the *umra* (the so-called minor pilgrimage, which includes the *tawwaf* and *sayy* rites only) during the months of Shawwal and Dhu al-Qa'dah, or the first seven days of Dhu al-Hijjah. Once the pilgrim completes the *umra*, he or she can exit *ihram* (for example, to visit Medina) and then reenter it on the eighth day of Dhu al-Hijjah with the intention of performing the hajj. A pilgrim need not return to a *miqaat* to reenter *ihram*, but can do so at his or her lodgings in Mecca or Mina. This type of hajj, which is considered the best by many Islamic scholars, requires a *hadi* to commemorate the *Eid al-Adha.*

—In the *qiraan*, one enters *ihram* for the purpose of performing hajj and *umra* together. The pilgrim's *ihram* is uninterrupted until he or she casts pebbles on the first day of the *eid* and (for a man) shaves his head. This type of hajj, which is the most common, also requires a *hadi.*

—In the *ifraad*, one enters *ihram* for the purpose of performing hajj only. No *hadi* is required. This type of hajj is available only to those who have completed a *tamattu'* or *qiraan* pilgrimage previously. It is performed primarily by Hejazis and is known locally as the Jeddah or "commuter" hajj.

After entering *ihram*, a pilgrim recites one time "O God! Here I am responding to you in performing the hajj (or *umra* and hajj, if one is *qiraan* pilgrim). O God! This hajj of mine is free from hypocrisy and boasting." Thereafter, the pilgrim continuously recites a verse called the *talbiyyah* until he or she begins casting pebbles at the *jamaraat* on the tenth day of Dhu al-Hijjah. It goes, "Here I am, O God, here am I. There is no partner with You. Here am I. Surely, all praise and graces are with You, and so is the dominion! There is no partner with You."

The first rite, the *tawwaf,* consists of circumambulating the Kaaba seven times. A pilgrim should approach Mecca from the upper (western) side, if possible, during daylight. He or she should enter the Grand Mosque through the al-Salaam Gate (also known as the Bani

Shaybah Gate). While doing so, the pilgrim recites, "I begin with the name of God. May God render his Messenger safe from every evil. O God! Open for me the gates of your mercy." Once he or she sees the Kaaba, the pilgrim should raise his hands and say, "O God! Greet us with peace."

The *tawwaf* should be undertaken immediately, unless it is time for congregational (Friday midday) prayers, in which case the pilgrim must first pray. The circumambulation starts with the kissing or touching (if possible) of the black stone embedded in the Kaaba's eastern corner. Otherwise, it is enough to point toward it while reciting, "In the name of God, God is greater" (the *takbir*).[5] The pilgrim proceeds counter-clockwise, repeating the *takbir* each time he or she passes before the black stone (marked by a black line on the white marble pavers of the plaza surrounding the Kaaba). In addition, the pilgrim should acknowledge the Kaaba's southern or Yemeni corner by touching it (again, if possible) and reciting, "Our Lord! Grant us the reward of a good action in this world and protect us from the torment of the fire."

After completing seven rounds, the pilgrim performs a two-*rak'aat* (prostrations) prayer, if possible, behind the Maqam Ibrahim—which Muslims believe is the rock upon which Ibrahim (Abraham) stood to rebuild the Kaaba with the help of his eldest son, Ismail (Ishmael)—or anywhere in the Grand Mosque. During the first *rak'ah* (prostration), he or she recites Al-Fatiha and Al-Kafiroon (the first and 109th *surahs*, or chapters, of the Qur'an) and, during the second *rak'ah*, Al-Fatiha and Al-Ikhlaas (the Qur'an's 112th *surah*) are recited. Following prayers, the pilgrim proceeds to Zam-Zam Well (located beneath the plaza to the northeast) and drinks as much of the holy water as he or she can and pours some on his or her head. The pilgrim then should leave the plaza for the long, two-level corridor where the *sayy* is performed.

On the way to the starting point of the *sayy* at the hillock al-Safa, the pilgrim recites, "verily, al-Safa and al-Marwa are among the rites of God, so there is no sin upon him who performs the hajj or the *umra* to walk back and forth between them. And whoever does good voluntarily, then verily God is appreciative and all-knowing." Once al-Safa is reached, the pilgrim recites, "I start with what God started." He or she then faces the Kaaba and repeats the *takbir* three times, followed by three recitations of "there is no true god except God alone. He fulfilled His promise and made His slave prevail, and He defeated the clans all alone."

The pilgrim next descends al-Safa and proceeds to al-Marwa, a distance of approximately 500 meters. Upon reaching al-Marwa, he or she walks up the hillock and makes the same supplications as atop al-Safa. This process is repeated until the pilgrim has made seven one-way trips. It is a *sunna* (a tradition derived from the practice of the Prophet) to jog or walk briskly a portion of the first three lengths and then take the last four at a leisurely pace.

In terms of tracking the hajj rites by the days, on the eighth day of Dhu al-Hijjah, known as the Day of Tarawih (comfort), the pilgrim performing *tamattu'* reenters *ihram*. A pilgrim staying in the Mecca area enters into *ihram* at his or her residence. Both should recite, "here am I responding to You, O God!" *Qarin* (a person performing the *qiraan* hajj) and *mufrid* (a person performing the *ifraad* hajj) pilgrims, because they have remained in *ihram*, commence with reciting the *talbiyyah*. If the pilgrim wishes to stipulate a conditional hajj, he or she should do so now. All pilgrims proceed to Mina before noon. There they should perform the five daily prayers at the appointed times, but shorten the *dhuhr* (midday), *'asr* (afternoon), and *isha'* (evening) prayers to two *rak'aat* each.

On the ninth day of Dhu al-Hijjah, known as the Day of Standing, the rising sun illuminates the procession of pilgrims to Arafat as they recite the *talbiyyah* and *takbir*. After reaching their camps, pilgrims perform the *dhuhr* and *'asr* prayers together, with two *rak'aat* each, at *dhuhr* prayer time. It is a *sunna* to spend the day as close as possible to Jabal al-Rahmah (a feat, given the crowds, that is impossible for most), facing the *qibla* (direction of prayer) and supplicating God with upturned palms while reciting, "there is no god but God alone. To Him belongs the dominion and all the praise is due Him, and He is capable of doing all things."

A pilgrim need not remain standing the entire day. One is permitted to sit or lie down, so long as he or she continues to supplicate God until sunset. It is unlawful to leave Arafat before sunset; if one does, he or she has invalidated his or her hajj and committed a sin. Once the sun sets, pilgrims are supposed to move calmly out of Arafat back to Muzdalifah (in practice, this so-called "rushing forth" frequently devolves into a frenzied stampede). There they perform *maghrib* prayers with three *rak'aat* and later the *isha'* prayer with two *rak'aat*. Pilgrims, except for the infirm and those assisting them, spend the night at camps in Muzdalifah.

The tenth of Dhu al-Hijjah, known as the Day of the Sacrifice, is celebrated throughout the Muslim world as the start of the *Eid al-Adha* (Feast of the Sacrifice). At the hajj, pilgrims arise at dawn to perform *fajr* prayers with four *rak'aat*. They then move to an open area called al-Mash'ar al-Haram and recite "there is no god but God alone. He has no partner and the dominion is His alone."

At sunrise, the pilgrims head back to Mina while reciting the *talbiyyah*. On the way, they collect seven chickpea-size pebbles. It is permissible to have gathered these in Muzdalifah or to wait and gather them once Mina is reached.

The pilgrims gather at al-Aqabah, the smallest and westernmost *jamrah* for the lapidation ritual. They cast their seven pebbles at it while shouting the *takbir* with each throw. Each pebble should fall into the basin surrounding the pillar; if it does not, another should be thrown in its place. It is forbidden to throw large stones, shoes, or other objects at the pillar, or to force one's way through to the front of the crowd.

After the lapidation, each pilgrim slaughters a *hadi* or (in the vast majority of cases nowadays) turns in a previously purchased certificate showing he or she has paid to have an animal (usually a sheep) slaughtered in his or her name. If one cannot afford the offering (the going rate is around $100), he or she should observe three days of fasting during the hajj and seven more after returning home.

Male pilgrims subsequently have their hair cut. According to a *sunna*, Muhammad invoked God's mercy three times on those among his followers who shaved their heads. It is sufficient for women to trim a small lock of hair.

At this point, a pilgrim may begin to withdraw from the state of ritual purity. All things that were prohibited are lawful again, except for sexual activity. This is known as the preliminary termination of *ihram*. The pilgrim next bathes and returns to Mecca to perform obligatory *tawwaf* (which may be done in his or her normal clothes). This is followed by a two-*rak'aat* prayer at Maqam Ibrahim (if possible) or anywhere else in the Grand Mosque.

If the pilgrim is performing *tamattu'* hajj, he or she must perform another *sayy*. *Qarins* and *mufrids* who did not perform the *sayy* following their arrival *tawwaf* must do so now. At this point, the hajj is ended and the pilgrim has reached the final termination of *ihram*. Sexual activity now is lawful. It is preferable to perform the *eid* rites in the prescribed order (lapidation, slaughter animal, cut or shave off hair, obligatory *tawwaf*, and the *sayy*) because that is the sequence the Prophet followed. However, no harm is done if a pilgrim performs one rite before another, such as cutting his or her hair before sacrificing the *hadi*, or performing *tawwaf* before casting the pebbles.

During days 11, 12, and 13 of Dhu al-Hijjah, pilgrims return to Mina to spend the *eid* holiday and perform the five daily prayers, shortening the four-*rak'aat* prayers (*dhuhr*, *'asr*, and *isha'*) to two *rak'aat* each. On the eleventh day, pilgrims cast seven pebbles at the easternmost *jamrah* (al-Kubra, located near the al-Khayf Mosque) in the same manner as they did the first pillar. Afterward, they step forward, keeping the *jamrah* on the left while facing the *qibla*, and supplicate God for at least 15 minutes. They then move on to lapidate (again with seven pebbles) the middle and largest *jamrah*, step aside (keeping the pillar on the right while facing the *qibla*), and supplicate God for at least 10 minutes. Finally, pilgrims return to the al-Aqabah (westernmost) *jamrah* and cast seven final pebbles. No supplications occur after this.

The lapidations may be repeated on the twelfth and thirteenth days of Dhu al-Hijjah. Indeed, it is permissible to delay casting the pebbles until the thirteenth day provided that the pilgrim lapidates in the proper sequence (easternmost *jamrah*, then the middle one, then al-Aqabah). When a pilgrim decides to leave Mina, he or she must—if not a resident of the area encompassed by the *mawaqeet*—return to the Grand Mosque and perform the farewell *tawwaf*.

There are a number of other points pilgrims should bear in mind when performing the hajj:

—Deputation for casting the pebbles is permissible only for weak or infirm, not healthy, men and women. A deputy must cast his or her pebbles first.

—A pilgrim is to refrain from lying, slander, and argument.

—One should choose good company and make sure the funds he or she brings are sufficient and that they were acquired through honest means.

—It is permissible for the *muhrim* (a person in the state of ihram) to bathe and wash his or her garments (or change into a clean set). He or she must use only unscented soap or laundry detergent.

—The period during which animals may be sacrificed extends until sunset of the thirteenth day of Dhu al-Hijjah.

—A menstruating woman or postnatal woman may perform the farewell *tawwaf*. However, the Prophet gave such women permission to leave without performing it.

Up to 75 percent of pilgrims, including most of those from abroad, visit Medina during the hajj. About half go before the pilgrimage rites begin, the rest after they are concluded. While in Medina, it is traditional to visit the Prophet's Mosque, pray in it, and greet God's Messenger. Many visitors also perform *wudhu'* at the nearby Quba'a Mosque (which marks the spot where Muhammad first prayed in Medina following his flight from Mecca) and perform two *rak'aat* there. Going to the Prophet's Mosque for the sole purpose of visiting Muhammad's grave is sinful, as are facing his tomb while praying or addressing him in supplications. Such acts are considered *shirk* (polytheism or associating others with God), the worst offense a Muslim can commit.

Mecca Prepares for Pilgrims (January 2002)

On January 23, 2002, I paid a call on the Hajj Ministry office or "establishment" responsible for Americans performing the pilgrimage. It comprises a central office and eight storefront facilities arrayed along Abdallah ibn Al-Zubayr Street, about 3 kilometers north of the Grand Mosque. They are identifiable by red-and-white signs and the numbers 31 through 38. The Ministry breaks down pilgrims on the basis of what are presumed to be shared cultural affinities. Americans, together with Western Europeans, Australians, and Turks, are handled by the division whose color theme is red. Within this division, each nationality is assigned a coordination/assistance establishment and a group of numbers corresponding to specific facilities.

Following tea and pleasantries, Khalid bin Muhammad Mujallid, the deputy director of the establishment, said that preparations for this year's pilgrimage have been proceeding very smoothly. He admitted he initially feared that the catastrophe of September 11 would negatively affect the number of visitors, particularly those coming from the West. In fact, he asserted, the tour companies are making bookings for numbers similar to those witnessed last year. Mujallid stated that he thought some 6,500 American citizens would arrive on U.S. passports to perform the hajj, with perhaps another 2,500 "dual national" Americans electing to use other passports for entry.

According to Mujallid, the new regulations holding tour companies more strictly accountable for the pilgrims they bring in for hajj (and *umra*) are enabling the Ministry to greatly streamline in-processing procedures. Relying on data compiled by the companies, Saudi authorities now are able to check in visitors once they reach their camps in Mina or their hotels in Mecca rather than having to halt buses outside the holy city to inspect documents. In effect, Mujallid said, the rules

60   Twilight in the Kingdom

have shifted the responsibility for obtaining the proper approvals—including visas—from the pilgrims to the tour companies. He continued that the Ministry, partly out of security concerns, is being very tough with the tour companies and will levy fines of up to 10 thousand riyals ($2,666.67) for each person they accept without adequate documentation or who fails to report for departure at the conclusion of the hajj.

Twenty or so minutes into our conversation, a harried looking American Muslim tour company operator entered the office wielding a half-inch-thick sheaf of papers. He hastily introduced himself and explained that he had arrived in the Kingdom 10 days earlier to ensure all was in order concerning a group of 100 New York pilgrims he will bring to Mecca on February 9. Not bothering to conceal his irritation, he said that the new regulations have made his life very difficult. He added that he flew from JFK to Jeddah last month to try to get the ball rolling with the required documentation, only to discover that the Saudis were not yet ready to deal with hajj paperwork. Now that they are, he fumed, he has precious little time to get all the signatures needed. As he angrily explained that he would be sued if he were unable to fulfill his promises to his clients, Mujallid paged an assistant, who produced a stack of signed documents. Mujallid calmly handed these to the tour company operator, stating he was free to go and bring in his "guests." The American sheepishly thanked the Deputy Director and scuttled out of the office.

Over lunch at an upscale Mecca hotel serving as the local headquarters of another tour company that brings thousands of Americans to Saudi Arabia each year for hajj, the company's Egyptian operations manager told me that the new paperwork requirements indeed are a chore. However, in his view, the procedures indicate the Saudis are becoming more professional in their handling of visitors. He predicted that the plethora of forms generated by the computerized tracking and check-in systems being debuted this year would be reduced in subsequent years as the "bugs" are worked out. He went on to observe that his company, which has been handling American pilgrims since 1995, enjoys excellent relations with the Hajj Ministry and uses these relations to minimize potential problems. For example, the Egyptian explained, the Saudis incorporated his suggestion that pilgrims and their luggage always be transported together to prevent tempers from flaring when—as inevitably happens—bags being moved separately from their owners go astray.

Following lunch, the tour company operator provided me with an overview of the routines followed by his office and "control room" staffs at the hotel. At the pilgrimage's peak, he said, he will have approximately 200 persons (direct and local hires) working around the clock. While rhapsodizing about the importance of customer service, he stated that all too often his colleagues in the tourism industry adopt an adversarial relationship with the Saudis. The Hajj Ministry, he continued, is no model of efficiency, but—relative to the how the rest of the government works—it really does a pretty good job. The key, he said, is making contact with those officials who care and then earning their support by helping them to look good in front of their superiors. "This is playing the game," the Egyptian smiled. "Not everyone likes it, but this is how things get done here."

After taking leave of the tour company operator, I returned to Mujallid's office to accompany him on a tour of the holy city and the hajj ritual sites. Considerable last-minute work was under way. Roads in all locations were being patched, and in downtown Mecca some phone and power lines were being transferred from poles to underground conduits. Interestingly, as many as half the storefronts serving as long-distance call "cabins" had been converted into Internet cafes during the last year or so; the city's cosmopolitan atmosphere henceforth will be characterized as much by the tap, tap of keyboards as by the telephonic babble of a hundred-plus languages.

The pilgrim encampment at Mina, completed last year, remains an awesome sight, with phalanxes of cage-like, white-canopied, fire-resistant "tents" marching to the horizon. As with the service establishments in Mecca, color-coding is used to denote Mina's various districts (red for Westerners, blue for Africans, green for Arabs, yellow for Asians, etc.). The vast al-Khayf Mosque on the encampment's eastern edge has been enlarged by the addition of a new portico allowing worshippers to pray outdoors in the shade. The tarmac around it remains, however, a treacherous obstacle course of open trenches, Jersey barriers, and piles of gravel. I spotted one worker clearing debris from the basin in which is set Jamarat al-Aqabah, the largest and westernmost of the three pillars at which pilgrims are required to cast pebbles.

At Muzdalifah, the Namira Mosque sported a fresh coat of white paint and the dry desert air rang with jackhammers as workers installed rows of new drinking fountains and toilets. Nearby, a discreet sign indicated the location of the pilgrims' court and jail facility. Because

The vast pilgrim encampment at Mina comprises several hundred thousand flame-retardant, fiberglass-sheathed, steel-framed "tents" topped with air conditioners. (Author)

hajj is a commercial venture as well as a religious experience, and because many pilgrims travel with wads of cash versus credit cards, the event presents an irresistible opportunity for pickpockets and thieves. According to Mujallid, Egyptians historically have been particularly notorious offenders.

Arafat was reasonably quiet save for the buzzing of four or five for-hire all-terrain vehicles piloted by Somali youths at breakneck speeds around the base of Jabal al-Rahmah. The ramparts of the "mountain" (a rocky hill, really) were besieged by the usual army of beggars, trinket vendors, and South Asian pilgrims who appear to hold the site in special reverence. Indeed, on the wide steps near the top, a clot of two dozen Afghans listened intently to an imam describe the farewell sermon the Prophet Muhammad delivered there in 632. A Sudanese man in a dirty gown hawked red-and-white checked *ghutras* (Bedouin headdresses) as a dromedary, decked out in a garish saddle and bridle, perched in magnificent incongruity next to his dozing Pakistani trainer. A handwritten sign reading "five riyals per ride" was propped against the whitewashed, 7-meter-high obelisk marking the summit proper.

The summit of Jabal al-Rahmah, inaccessible during the crush and chaos of the hajj, is a placid tourist trap the rest of the year. (Author)

A Pilgrim's Journal (February 2002)

I participated in the hajj under the auspices of the Saudi Arabian National Guard (SANG). I and other SANG guests were required to assemble at noon on February 20 at Jeddah's Marriott hotel. The atmosphere in the dimly lit lobby was one of great anticipation; gaggles of *ihram*-clad men milled about excitedly with their wives and children in tow as SANG personnel circulated answering questions and pleading for patience with those who were most anxious to get on the road to Mecca. Bus assignments were made, pilgrims were introduced to the SANG officers responsible for them, and—at last—boarding commenced at two o'clock. A pudgy, jocular young lieutenant commander with spectacularly bad teeth (apparently owing to his fondness for extra-sweet tea) explained to me and the other passengers on bus number four that, unfortunately, the vehicle's air conditioning was broken. Moreover, he continued, the SANG had more guests than it had anticipated, so everyone would have to crowd together; a Blue Bird school bus designed to transport 40 children was made to accommodate 50 sweaty adults and several minors along with all their luggage.

The lieutenant commander shortly was joined by a grinning non-commissioned officer (NCO) assistant and a hunched, long-limbed SANG driver. With the boarding process finally completed at 2:45, the five buses pulled out and headed east. The lieutenant commander led the bus-four passengers in reciting the *talbiyyah*, and the air wafting through the open windows helped to ameliorate what had become a sauna-like atmosphere. As the SANG convoy sailed through the five checkpoints on the highway (passing no fewer than 27 Defense Ministry buses ferrying troops to police the holy sites), one of my fellow passengers—a Saudi—compared the pilgrimage to an Outward Bound experience. The first challenge, and often the toughest for many, is simply getting there, he said. Although hardly a walk in the park, the SANG group's travails throughout the hajj would prove far easier than those of "ordinary" pilgrims.

Utilizing special tunnels closed to all but official traffic, the SANG buses pulled into the station beneath the Grand Mosque shortly before afternoon prayers at about 3:45. The passengers alighted, made their ablutions in the washroom complexes one level up, and ascended to the vast plaza. As the prayer call rang out, several of my bus-four companions and I found open space amid the detritus of the hajj (empty water bottles, fast food wrappers, and other assorted trash) to say our prayers. We then approached the mosque, stowed our sandals, and entered to perform the arrival *tawwaf* and the *sayy*.

The lieutenant commander and the other SANG officers had informed their charges that we were to be back on the buses at 6:00 sharp. As I joined the hundreds of thousands circumambulating the Kaaba at a glacial crawl, I wondered whether there would be enough time to complete the *tawwaf*, much less the *sayy*. However, once I moved past the starting point at the black-stone corner (denoted by a dark stripe embedded in the cool, white marble pavers), the pace picked up. Indeed, as I moved toward the perimeter to facilitate a faster clip for the first three laps (a *sunna* of the Prophet), I nearly was run over by a train of litter-bearers carrying elderly and infirm persons. Each wooden palanquin was supported by four African men with thick cotton pads on their heads. Paid by the pilgrim, they moved with remarkable speed around the shrine, sweating profusely and shouting at people to get out of the way. Although the crowd for the most part was well-behaved and did not push, several cannonball-like Turkish babushkas apparently had not been informed that the hajj is an occasion for civility. They chucked their way viciously against the flow of traffic in what one could only surmise was a desperate search for lost family members.

With the arrival *tawwaf* completed, my companions and I attempted to pray at the Maqam Ibrahim (easier said than done, given the constant flow of pilgrims into and out of circumambulation) and then descended to the Zam-Zam well complex to refresh ourselves with holy water. Ascending once more, we made our way to the 500-meter-long corridor enclosing the hillocks of al-Safa and al-Marwa to perform the *sayy*. The beginning point atop al-Safa was so congested that getting through necessitated juking and jiving like Jim Brown. Brief supplications followed and then it was time to walk. From atop al-Safa, the corridor looked like a river of heads bobbing amid rapids of white terry cloth. Per a *sunna*, the first 150 meters or so from al-Safa to al-Marwa are to be jogged, with the result that an immense bottleneck formed halfway down the corridor that was relieved only as people came off of al-Marwa and began the trip back to al-Safa.

Most of the people I saw about me were young and able-bodied, belying the popular conception that the hajj is oversubscribed by those on death's doorstep. Nevertheless, an aisle running down the middle of the two one-way *sayy* lanes was chock-a-block full of wheelchair-bound penitents and the helpers who struggled to push them up the inclines at either end. While the *tawwaf* was characterized by the sounds of mumbled prayers and sliding feet punctuated by the chirps of dive-bombing swallows and the shouts of the litter-bearers, the *sayy*—being an indoor event—reverberated like a giant kazoo with the bedlam of nattering, hacking, and spitting pilgrims.

Following hurriedly performed *maghrib* (sunset) prayers, the SANG contingent reboarded the buses at 6:30 and waited, patiently, as one of the vehicles with a dead battery was jump-started by another. An hour later the group moved out for the SANG's encampment at Mina. Again utilizing tunnels reserved for official vehicles, the convoy reached the tent city (fewer than 10 kilometers away) in 45 minutes; pilgrims making the same trip on general-use roadways wound up stuck in massive traffic jams lasting several hours. Our drivers expertly threaded the school buses into the narrow compound and discharged their passengers. Tent assignments were announced by the lieutenant commander and the NCO and the pilgrims made their way to their digs.

The accommodations, simple but adequate, were luxurious compared with those afforded most hajj-goers. The floor of my "tent" (in reality an air-conditioned steel frame capped with a pointed fiberglass roof and sheathed in fire-resistant fabric panels) was covered in machine-made cotton kilms. Ten thin, foam mattresses (known locally as "Yemeni mats") were arrayed with new sheets, pillows, and blankets atop each. A cooler filled with sodas and bottled waters on ice reposed in a corner next to extra cases of soft drinks. Track lights clamped to the steel frame provided ample illumination. After resting for a time, my tent mates and I attended evening prayers at the nearby "mosque tent," ate (a plain but plentiful buffet) at the "dining tent," and obtained our SANG photo-ID cards enabling us to exit and reenter the compound. Situated near the Indian tent city on the central King Abd al-Aziz Road, the SANG's encampment is in one of the noisiest sections of Mina. The sounds, and smells, of diesel trucks idling through the night were accompanied by occasional screams of sirens, Saudi traffic police barking admonitions through bullhorns, and the roiling murmur of more than 2 million souls looking ahead to the Day of Standing.

At the conclusion of dawn prayers the following morning (Thursday, February 21), a guest imam from the Royal Saudi Land Forces (RSLF) seized the microphone and launched into an interminable explanation of the dos and don'ts of the Day of Standing. Bleary eyed pilgrims nodded mutely as he droned on. Some 45 minutes later he was still at it, although all but a handful of his audience had left to eat breakfast and pack essentials to take to Arafat. Amid the roar of thousands of vehicles, my companions and I boarded the SANG buses at 9:00 a.m. Because one of the five again would not start, its passengers were shoehorned into the other four, making an already hot and uncomfortable ride even more tortuous. With no "special roads" available for use, the convoy took to the central byway, with the result that the 11-kilometer trip took nearly two hours. On the way, I spied what appeared to be an aqueduct stretching for several kilometers along the hills north of Muzdalifah. The lieutenant commander identified it as the Bir Zubaydah and said it was the terminal portion of the Darb Zubaydah, an Abbasid-era pilgrim road featuring water channels and pools. No sooner had the buses disgorged their passengers at the Arafat pilgrim encampment (composed of older, stout canvas tents strewn haphazardly over the vast, gravely plain) than several of my companions decided to head for the Namira Mosque to secure a place to perform midday prayers.

We took one of several footpaths to Namira radiating from the mosque like spokes in a giant wheel. Pilgrims, some of whom clearly had been there for days, were squatting beneath makeshift shelters composed of tarpaulins suspended from plastic ropes tied between scrawny trees. Many male pedestrians carried umbrellas to shade their naked heads from the intense sunlight, while centipedal lines of tightly bundled Malaysian and Indonesian females snaked by, each pilgrim walking with her right hand on the shoulder of the woman in front of her. Namira, a hulking, no-frills, prefabricated shell, loomed ever closer. Mist supplied by sprinklers attached high on lampposts cooled us as we arrived at the concrete plaza surrounding the mosque. However, there proved to be no room for additional worshippers within the facility; RSLF troops waded into the throngs and forcibly ejected those who persisted in trying to gain entry. My disappointed companions and I returned to the SANG tents to pray and pass the remainder of the hot, breezy day there.

Following a catered lunch consisting of *kabsa* (mutton and rice) washed down with orange juice, the SANG contingent settled down to an afternoon of sweaty contemplation inside the stifling tents. Helicopters rasped incessantly in the skies above as some of the pilgrims read aloud from Qur'ans and prayer books. Others sat or lay groggily on the lumpy floor. As the sun began to set, a Syrian imam convinced some of the men to join him in standing outside to chant the *talbiyyah* and the *takbir*. Just before *maghrib* prayers, the lieutenant commander appeared and told his charges that it was time to go. Those wishing to pray would have to offer their supplications on the buses.

The "rushing forth" or exodus from Arafat to Muzdalifah engendered the largest traffic jam I have ever seen. Our buses, along with every other vehicle within a several-mile radius, idled at a standstill from 5:00 until after 7:30. Finally, at about 7:45, there was movement and the SANG drivers, clearly at their wits' end, gunned the Blue Birds through gaps in the congestion that appeared barely large enough to accommodate a Honda Civic. A pell-mell dash for the tunnels leading to Muzdalifah ensued, with the *talbiyyah* giving way to prayers for safety from my petrified fellow pilgrims. Noticing the ashen looks on our faces, the lieutenant commander chuckled and began describing in great detail some of the gruesome road accidents he had witnessed during previous pilgrimages.

The enervated SANG guests disembarked at a stand of smelly, moth-eaten tents in the geographic center of Muzdalifah. After combining sunset and evening prayers, several of us went out to find pebbles to use in the following day's lapidation ritual. Having succeeded in this endeavor, we were nearly not allowed back into the SANG compound; it was besieged by hundreds of pilgrims bearing slips of pink paper who claimed that Mecca Governor Prince Abd al-Majeed had given them permission to crash at the site for the evening. The SANG guards disavowed any knowledge of such an arrangement and were in the process of padlocking the gates when my companions and

I managed, after considerable shoving and shouting, to wheedle our way back in.

Among those I met in Muzdalifah was a London-based Iraqi dissident. He was invited by the National Guard to participate in the hajj as an official guest after he published a book claiming that Shia in Iran increasingly are abandoning the concept of *velayat-i faqih* ("the mandate of the jurist") in favor of the Sunni concept of *shura* (consultation) in governance. A Shia who once resided in Tehran (where he said he made anti-Saddam broadcasts on Arab radio and thus helped to precipitate the Iran-Iraq war) found numerous points of agreement with several Sudanese pilgrims of the moderate Hanafi school of Islamic jurisprudence, who were gently critical of the Kingdom's Hanbali-school inflexibility and Wahhabi obsession with following the *hadith* and *sunna* to the letter. The eldest of the Sudanese merrily observed that the Day of Standing in fact is the hajj; everything else merely is icing on the cake. Over another meal of mutton and rice served on a large aluminum platter set upon the uncomfortably hard floor of the tent, a strident young American pilgrim and his British sidekick argued with the Iraqi and the Sudanese that the only acceptable hajj is one modeled as closely as possible on the Prophet Muhammad's example. Several Yemenis, befitting their reputation as the pragmatists of the Arab world, tried unsuccessfully to stake out a middle ground that both sides could agree on.

The theological discussion wore on until 11:00 p.m., when the lieutenant commander appeared and announced that it was time again to board to buses—the group would be heading to the *jamaraat* to cast pebbles at the first (easternmost) of the devil-pillars, Jamarat al-Kubra, at Mina. In response to complaints from the young American, the Brit, and several others, the SANG official said that the *ulama* (Saudi Arabia's official clerical establishment) had issued a *fatwa* (legally binding religious injunction) allowing the stoning to begin with al-Kubra just after midnight, although the Prophet began with Jamarat al-Aqabah at midmorning. He continued that those who wanted were welcome to spend the night at Muzdalifah. However, they would have to find their own way back to the SANG encampment at Mina.

Several of the *sunna*-sticklers stayed, but all the other SANG guests boarded the buses for what turned out to be a fairly quick (90-minute) drive to Mina. Indeed, most of the time was spent simply trying to maneuver the Blue Birds out of the Muzdalifah tent city, where they had been hemmed in by dozens of Suburbans and Land Cruisers. The scene of the lapidations was one of pandemonium. In the yellowing

glare of huge floodlights, throbbing, chanting hordes of delirious pilgrims pressed forward around the circular base of the pillar to shower
it, as well as their fellows on all sides, with pebbles, rocks, and chunks
of concrete. I saw several bystanders stagger away holding their heads.
After managing to get in close enough to cast my pebbles and to retreat
without getting hit, I encountered two Afghans who congratulated me
on my throws. They asked my nationality in broken English and, upon
learning I was an American, commented that pilgrims from the United
States and Palestine make the best rock-tossers.

Upon returning to Mina at 3:00 a.m. on Friday, February 22, several
of my companions and I undertook a fruitless search for an all-night
barbershop in the tent city. We stumbled back to our Yemeni mats at
4:00 a.m. Dawn prayer came much too early, of course. Nonetheless,
most of my group did get up and pray, and nearly everyone who did
went back to sleep afterward. By 10:00, however, all had arisen, break-
fasted, and were eager to perform the *tawwaf al-ifadha*—the obligatory
circumambulation of the Kaaba on the occasion of the *Eid al-Adha*.
The lieutenant commander having informed the group the previous
evening that it henceforth was on its own in terms of transportation,
several of us caught a minibus (20 riyals for a seat inside, 10 for one on
the top) to the Grand Mosque.

The mosque was even more crowded than it had been two days
before. The plaza surrounding the Kaaba was stuffed suffocatingly full
of worshippers, and progress around the shrine was measured in centimeters. It took those who remained at the ground level more than
two-and-one-half hours to complete the *tawwaf.* I went up to the
mosque's roof, where a longer—but much speedier—circumambulation
was possible: Seven laps in fewer than 90 minutes. After exiting the
mosque and performing afternoon prayers outside, I strolled across the
street to check out two barbershops. Both had lines stretching for
blocks in one door and a steady stream of cue-balled pilgrims exiting
the other. Determined to find a less crowded salon, I wandered down
King Faysal street past innumerable shops selling worry beads, prayer
rugs, and other souvenirs. A young Indonesian man carrying a razor
emerged from an alley and whispered that he was giving haircuts.
Asked how much, he replied 10 riyals and said he changed blades
between customers. I followed him behind some shops to a small hill
carpeted in shorn locks. I sat on a three-legged stool and the
Indonesian lathered and shaved my head in fewer than 5 minutes.
With that I returned to Mina (by private hack; 10 riyals) to shower and
doff my *ihram* in favor of a *thobe*, the Saudi (male) national garb.

The remainder of the *eid* was spent relaxing in Mina. A few other members of the SANG group joined me in touring portions of the tent city, where we encountered Ethiopian women selling inexpensive clothing, Russians hawking carpets and pelts, and Pakistanis purveying cumin and other spices. Following *maghrib* prayers, I was informed by the lieutenant commander that I, along with a number of other SANG guests, were to be received by Crown Prince Abdallah, who was arriving in Mina that evening. At 9:00 I put on my dress *thobe* and joined the other special guests in a holding area before being escorted to the reception tent at 9:30. The other SANG invitees and I were seated on the left side of the aisle toward the back. The rows in front of us were reserved for more prominent guests, and the right side was filled with National Guard personnel. At about 10:30, a number of government officials, including Hajj Minister Madani, Mecca Governor Abd al-Majeed, General Intelligence Presidency Director Nawwaf, SANG Western Region Commander Faysal bin Abdallah, and SANG Assistant Deputy Commander Miteb bin Abdallah, arrived and seated themselves at the front of the room to the left of the Crown Prince's central armchair.

A few moments later, six members of the *ulama* filed in and sat in the front to the right of Abdallah's seat. Senior foreign diplomats, including the Iranian Ambassador, then entered and sat near the front; the latter exchanged baleful glares with some of the Saudi clerics. Madani invited one of his guests, the director of a Malaysian Islamic university, to sit next to him. Finally Abdallah, preceded by television cameras and clouds of incense, entered at 11:30 p.m. He walked slowly up the center aisle, turning to wave greetings to the now-standing audience on either side. Once he was seated and coffee was served, the SANG officers began organizing a receiving line. The lieutenant commander, along with his boss (a colonel), raced to the back of the tent, grabbed my arms, and escorted me to near the front of the queue, where I wound up being among the first presented to the Crown Prince. After all were once more seated, the Malaysian university director stumbled through a paean of praise for our host followed by an enthusiastic ode delivered in a lisping Najdi dialect by a SANG corporal. The reception then ended and Abdallah departed, followed by his guests.

Saturday, February 23, dawned clear and cool at Mina. After a hearty, Arab-style breakfast (beans, bread, beef bacon, and yogurt), my companions and I walked to the *jamaraat* to cast seven pebbles at each of the three devil-pillars. The approximately 7-kilometer hike took us past precipitous hillsides teeming with campers and large parking lots where mainly African and South Asian pilgrims were ensconced in mounds of trash. In some places the refuse was ankle deep, necessitating slow going. Trucks from various bottled water, soft drink, and snack food companies parked by an elevated road were overwhelmed by pilgrims seeking handouts. Several entrepreneurs squatted nearby selling to passersby what they had just received for free.

The *jamaraat* themselves were not crowded. My companion and I were able to approach close to the three pillars and cast seven stones at each in fewer than 15 minutes. We noticed that RSLF troops were holding back several large delegations of Indonesian and Indian pilgrims wishing to perform the lapidations *en masse*. According to a SANG officer on the scene, big groups in previous years had been the cause of deaths from crushing and stampedes, so the authorities were adamant about making sure all adhered to a predetermined timetable at the *jamaraat*. At least eight ambulances were standing by, however, and I saw a female pilgrim with a bloody face carried away on a stretcher.

We returned to our tent at midmorning. After thanking my SANG hosts for a memorable experience, and deputizing a companion to stone the three pillars for me once more the following day, I packed my bag and caught a minibus to the Grand Mosque. From there I hailed a cab home to Jeddah.

CHAPTER 4
God and Man

Pray as if everything depended on God and work
as if everything depended on man.
                    —Francis Cardinal Spellman

The devil, so the saying goes, is in the details. Perhaps it must follow
that God is in the big picture, the forest we cannot see for the trees, the
desert horizon missed while staring at the dunes. No people I've ever
met, including evangelical American Protestants, are as fixated on the
Supreme Being and the hereafter as are the Saudis. Hejazis, owing I
suspect to the presence of the two holy cities so close by, are particularly afflicted by the need to contemplate, and in some way resonate
with, the divine. It is as if the land on which they were born and
raised, the very molecules of their being make it inevitable for all—the
most secular-minded included—to define themselves in ways that only
the truly God-fearing (and, in some cases, God-loathing) can.

The Hejazi contemplation of God is no mere navel-gazing exercise.
Taught from a young age that history ended with the appearance of
the Prophet, and that all that has happened in the world in the 14 centuries since is merely a prelude to the End of Days, Saudis in the Hejaz
should, by rights, rank among the world's most fatalistic people. But
they are not fatalists. Many are, of course, given to explaining the tri-
als and tribulations of their lives as manifestations of divine will, but
my experiences in the Hejaz taught me that most are not at all averse
to moving heaven and earth, if necessary, to get themselves and their

families ahead in the here-and-now. Fatalism serves as a convenient crutch for those too lazy to exert themselves or simply too beaten down by time and circumstances to try or to care any longer. It also comes in handy as perhaps the most socially acceptable, if frequently unstated, excuse in a land where decades of totalitarianism have made all but the most foolhardy gun-shy of accepting responsibility for anything. The upshot is that, for Saudis on the make, there is no need to fear failure or to feel ashamed if a crackpot scheme goes awry. Fault, like responsibility, goes up the ladder, not down, and an ample pantheon composed of royal family members, wealthy merchants, and foreign big shots exists, seemingly—to the proverbial man-in-the-street, at least—for the sole purpose of absorbing and diffusing the failings of lesser beings. Of course, greater calamities involving nature, death, and disease remain the province of God proper, liberating the lame (and, not incidentally, the drunk driver who made him so) from blame.

Getting and staying ahead, with or without God's help or approval, is the true driver of the Hejazi psyche. In this way my Saudi friends reminded me of Americans. Most were not hard workers of the type one sees in any U.S. enterprise. Few would last a day in a fast-paced Los Angeles law office, let alone exhibit the moxie needed to rise from cleaning the partners' homes to managing a custodial business. But the restlessness, the never-ending search for the next foothold on the imaginary wall of success, these characteristics—coupled with a God-fearing exterior and a perpetual, Scarlet O'Hara-like optimism that something better must be coming down the pike—helped me to see that there is little, really, separating the young Saudi male dreaming his life away sipping tea and surfing pornography in a dark, Jeddah Internet café and his American peer struggling to pay the bills while working days in a corporate mailroom and completing his degree at night.

This chapter includes six reports in which I attempted to explain the Hejazi conception of where preordination leaves off and human attempts to affect outcomes begin. The first covers the controversial subject of magic, one means by which Saudis I knew sought to assert control over their own, and sometimes others', destinies. The second provides a glimpse into how the law—as in the West—functions as a channel for exercising and controlling human desires. Unlike in Europe and the United States, however, the Saudi legal system is imbued with, and often trumped by, religious sentiments that have little or nothing to do with secular jurisprudence. The third report is an account of a visit by an official U.S. delegation that sought to engage Saudi religious and political leaders on the subject of religious freedom (or, more accurately, the lack thereof) in the Kingdom. The fourth tackles the thorny issue of how Islamic shibboleths are interpreted, long a source of contention within and without the Hejaz. In this report, I sought to point out how an accepted "given," forming the basis on which assumptions about what is and what is not permissible in the Kingdom, is not nearly as rock solid as our Saudi interlocutors would have us believe. The fifth report delves into the gray zone between God and man to outline a cosmology we in the West might find absurdly irrational, one by which my contacts nevertheless set great store. The sixth report takes a different tack, tracing the historic roots of intolerance in Saudi Arabia—something many Hejazis refuse to recognize—from the advent of Islam to its full flowering in Wahhabism.

Magic (April 2000)

Perhaps because magic was important in the belief systems of pre-Islamic Arabia, it is mentioned in the Qur'an as a real (and evil) phenomenon. Indeed, the stories of the miracles wrought by the prophets to convince the nonbelievers are the only instances in which magic is cast in a positive light. What passes for magic nowadays frequently involves fortunetelling with tea leaves and coffee grounds, a popular and socially acceptable form of entertainment among local ladies. Occasionally, the Hejazi press features stories about gullible Saudis being swindled out of handsome sums by con artists posing as magicians. The stratagems of these supposed miracle workers—invariably identified as foreigners—vary, but a common element in each tale is the overweening greed of the victim.

In a recent *Okaz*[1] article, for example, an Algerian man promised to double the money of a Saudi burgher in Jeddah by chanting snatches of the Qur'an over a box of cash buried in the ground. The Saudi put 1,000 riyals (about $267) in the box and allowed the Algerian to bury it in his yard and recite several bits of scripture. When he and the Algerian unearthed the box the next day, it contained 2,000 riyals. Emboldened by this apparent success, the man put 5,000 riyals in the box. The same routine was followed, and when it was dug up the box was revealed to contain 10,000 riyals. Convinced of the magician's powers, the Saudi reportedly placed his life's savings, totaling some 300,000 riyals, into the box. He watched eagerly as it was buried, listened raptly to the Algerian's sonorous incantations, and went happily home to dream of a doubled fortune. Not surprisingly, he returned the following morning to find a hole in the ground and no trace of the supposed magician.

While avarice keeps local magicians busy, self-styled faith healers in the Hejaz minister to the lovesick. For centuries, Hejazi women have hired imams (prayer leaders) and *khatibs* (Muslim cantors) to recite Qur'anic verses in efforts to keep their husbands from taking new brides or to revive the passion in their marriages (a challenge increasingly met by Viagra vice prayer). Meanwhile, several of my contacts report that, in the last few years, single young Saudi men with good jobs and disposable incomes have taken to paying un- and underemployed university friends who majored in Qur'anic studies to conduct prayer services aimed at making them irresistible to the opposite sex. Although all involved understand that these Hejazi urban professionals are after nothing more than a bit of slap and tickle, the effort is billed as a means of facilitating marriage, thus ensuring that the young Islamic scholars are not blamed for providing the services.

Desperate Hejazis sometimes turn to faith-healing for problems that cannot otherwise be remedied. A stay-at-home Jeddah mom told me that her neighbors locked their 10-year-old retarded son alone in his room for nearly a week without food or water because a renowned imam from Qassim (a Najdi governorate regarded as the heartland of Wahhabism) had convinced them that God would help the boy if they did so. Of course, no miracle occurred and the traumatized child spent a month in the hospital recovering while the imam was never heard from again (at least not in Jeddah). Other examples of "magical thinking" abound: The managing partner of a local travel and tourism firm reported that the former wife of a wealthy businessman here spent thousands of riyals on spells peddled by itinerant Islamic faith healers who claimed they could make her husband fall in love with her again. A pilot trainer at Saudi Arabian Airlines told me that a young male passenger recently suffered an epileptic seizure on a domestic flight. The plane's copilot, trained as a paramedic, rushed to the man's seat, cleared his airway, and prevented him from injuring himself, while a fellow passenger—an imam from Riyadh—prayed loudly from across the aisle. The young man recovered, and when the jet landed in Jeddah it was the imam, not the quick-thinking copilot, who was lauded for saving a life.

Under *Sharia* (Islamic law), the practice of magic is regarded as the worst kind of *shirk* (polytheism), an offense for which no repentance is accepted and that is punishable by death. Stories concerning magic and faith-healing in the Hejaz can be amusing or pathetic in their turn, but some can have serious consequences, particularly when reputations or societal mores are harmed. In February, *Al-Bilad*[2] reported that the Interior Ministry had ordered the execution of a Sudanese man convicted of "sorcery." The man claimed to be an herbalist and had treated a number of Hejazi matrons with tonics and potions; a search of his dwelling revealed that he possessed some 16 spell books and related paraphernalia. *Al-Bilad* noted that he confessed to conspiring with *jinn* (identified in Muslim belief as beings made of smokeless fire who coexist with humans) in "efforts to separate wives from their husbands," a delicate way of stating that he seduced his married clients.

In the Islamic cosmology, *jinn* are key players whose existence helps to explain the otherwise inexplicable. According to the imam of a small Jeddah mosque, *jinn* can be both good and bad (unlike angels, beings of light, who always are good). They assume a variety of guises: Some appear as black cats, snakes, scorpions, and dogs (many Muslims believe angels will not enter a home where a dog is present); some manifest themselves as the wind; and some can be recognized as people with oddly incandescent eyes. They affect events and lives, frequently in negative ways. Evil *jinn* delight in exploiting human weaknesses and are quick to latch onto people who are impassioned easily. For example, said the imam, it is commonly believed in the Hejaz that the influence of *jinn* explains why Saudi men are drawn to Moroccan women (he claimed a disproportionate number of Hejazis have taken Moroccan brides through the years). Other contacts say it is widely accepted that Jewish women (who, during the time of the Prophet, were feared as "blowers in knots," that is, sorceresses) conspire with *jinn* to entrap Muslim men in compromising affairs.

The most prevalent of all magical beliefs here is the evil eye. On one level, it is similar to the ancient Greek concept of hubris, in which the gods smote mortals for exhibiting pride or arrogance. Unlike hubris, however, the evil eye is a product of envy, enabling one to fall victim to it through no fault of his or her own. For example, when the visitor to a home comments on its beauty without stating *masha'allah, tabarak allah* (a formula which ascribes all good fortune to God rather than to human efforts), he or she invokes the wrath of the evil eye upon the dwelling's occupants. Similarly, one should always take care to say *masha'allah* rather than directly praise another's child; should the child become sick or die, the parent could hold the praising party responsible.

Sometimes it is possible to inflict the evil eye unintentionally, such as when one cannot keep him- or herself from feeling jealous of another's success, spouse, or possessions. In such cases, according to a Western-educated *da'wa* (Islamic proselytizing) official in Jeddah, one should take seven leaves from the *sidir* tree (a type of desert thorn bush), crush and brew a tea with them, then drink the infusion while reciting the second and longest *surah* of the Qur'an, "The Cow." To ward off the evil eye, many Hejazis—in contravention of Wahhabi dictates—carry small, eye-shaped amulets; inscribe *masha'allah, tabarak allah* on the lintels of their homes; or hang fist-size salt crystals in their windows (believing that the crystals shrink over time as they counteract envy). Those who are more inclined to hew to Wahhabi orthodoxy make a habit of reciting the Qur'an's *surahs* 113 ("Daybreak") and 114 ("Mankind") before going to bed.

While views about the dangers of magic in general vary, my contacts are unanimous in describing black magic, or witchcraft, as the most potent and serious kind of sorcery. It is a topic many are reluctant to discuss, both because it is un-Islamic (indeed, it is regarded by Wahhabis as anti-Islamic) and for fear of arousing the ire of evil *jinn*. Nonetheless, several shared with me examples of the forms and uses of Islamic witchcraft, a number of which involve the Qur'an:

—Qur'anic verses can be recited backwards to cause one's enemies to fail in their endeavors.

—Qur'anic verses can be written in menstrual blood to cause a rival female to become barren.

—Qur'anic verses can be written in semen to cause a rival male to become impotent.

—Qur'anic verses can be written in excrement to cause an intended victim to fall ill. Alternatively, a piece of the intended victim's clothing can be tied into knots to cause abdominal pain.

—A Qur'anic verse can be written in a square upon the palm of a child's left hand; misfortune accompanies the child when he or she enters the home of the intended victim.

—Qur'anic verses can be written on a piece of paper soaked in human urine and dried, which is then burned and the ashes mixed with the intended victim's food (this is alleged to bring death within 48 hours). Similarly, a chameleon can be dried, crushed, and mixed with the victim's food to produce a life-threatening fever.

Hejazis who believe themselves to be the intended victims of black magic have several defenses available. The most Islamically correct is to engage an imam or *khatib* to perform what amounts to an exorcism by reciting the entire Qur'an while moving from room to room within the client's home through the course of one evening. This ceremony is said to be most effective on the nights marking the beginning and the end of the lunar month. Tradition holds that it may not be performed during the fasting month of Ramadan.

A less conventional preventive measure is to leave a Qur'an in the home open to *surah* 2 ("The Cow"), verse 102, which reads as follows:

And they followed instead what the devils had recited during the reign of Solomon. It was not Solomon who disbelieved, teaching people magic and that which was revealed to the two angels at Babylon, Harut and Marut. But they (the two angels) do not teach anyone unless they say "we are a trial, so do not disbelieve (by practicing magic)." And yet they learn from them that by which they cause separation between a man and his wife. But they do not harm anyone through it except by permission of God. And they (people) learn what harms them and does not benefit them. But they (the children of Israel) certainly knew that whoever purchased it (magic) would not have in the Hereafter any share. And wretched is that for which they sold themselves, if only they knew.

According to contacts familiar with the habits of rural Hejazis, it remains the custom of Bedouin women to carry inscriptions of Qur'anic verses (especially from *surah* 105, "The Elephant") in vials or phylacteries that often are crafted into necklaces. This is believed to reduce the potency of evil spells and curses, while discouraging the *jinn* from making mischief.

Because faith outweighs reason in the minds of many Muslims, the importance of magical thinking should not be underestimated by Westerners wishing to understand what might otherwise appear as irrational or irresponsible behaviors in the Hejaz. Rather than devote their energies to grappling scientifically with life's mysteries, religious Hejazis have adopted a philosophical approach based on the idea that an all-knowing God reveals to humans only what He wishes. Life and death, good and evil, reason and faith, all are encompassed by the ubiquitous phrase *insha'allah*: If God wills it. For those unwilling to wait for the divine plan to be made manifest, magic represents a direct, if perilous, channel through which the Almighty's will may be discerned and, perhaps, influenced.

Lawyers, Courts, and Sharia (June 2000)

Lawyering is a young profession in the Hejaz. Jeddah's King Abd al-Aziz University (KAAU) inaugurated its law faculty only a decade ago. Until then, most run-of-the-mill cases were handled by amateurs who, if their clients were fortunate, acquired certificates of competency in *Sharia* before hanging out their shingles. High-profile legal actions were entrusted to Arab expatriate solicitors, mainly Egyptians. Although foreigners continue to play an important role here, particularly with regard to international trade and investment disputes, the early graduates of KAAU's five-year law program now dominate the legal sector.

The Jeddah Lawyers Association has 2,000 or so members on its roster. A few are big-name hotshots, such as Salah al-Hejailan, the brother of the Gulf Cooperation Council Secretary General and the defendants' attorney in the celebrated case of two British nurses accused of murdering an Australian colleague several years ago. In general, however, to be a Saudi lawyer is to labor in obscurity. Most do not realize tremendous wealth or social status, much less inspire contempt. Indeed, local barristers can only dream of attracting the peculiar admixture of derision and envy Americans attach to their legal eagles.

Most of Jeddah's lawyers are sole practitioners. Among the few large firms, there are several of note besides al-Hejailan's firm. One of these is the quaintly named International House of Law (IHL), a five-lawyer general practice founded in 1996 by 30-something partners Khalid Abu Rashed and Hassan Dahlan. I met Abu Rashed at the home of one of his clients, Prince Faysal bin Thamer, who oversees security in Mecca Governorate (within which Jeddah is located). Abu Rashed subsequently treated me to a tour of IHL's offices and arranged for me to accompany him to a *Sharia* court session in Jeddah.

During my visit to IHL's offices on the morning of June 25, Abu Rashed told me that the entirety of the Kingdom's laws and regulations theoretically fall within the purview of *Sharia*, or Islamic law. In practice, however, pure *Sharia* is used only to adjudicate family law and criminal cases. Everything else is subsumed within three other areas of law: administrative, labor, and banking and finance. There obviously is considerable overlap among these artificial divisions, Abu Rashed continued, but a case normally is handled by the court most relevant to the core issue. For example, a case touching on *Sharia* that is at root a labor dispute will be handled by the labor court, while a financial matter involving theft will be assigned to the *Sharia* court's docket.

Jeddah's judicial complex is located on a sprawling compound that, until eight years ago, was the site of Crown Prince Abdallah's villa. The main building houses the court's presidency and its administrative apparatus. There are 25 smaller cottage and former guest houses, each of which has been converted into a combination courtroom and judge's chambers. A single jurist presides at each. Eleven of the 25 courtrooms deal exclusively with *Sharia* issues. Administrative, labor, and banking/financial cases are parceled out more or less evenly among the other 14 courtrooms.

Saudi judges are the lords of their domains. They are appointed by the Royal Diwan (the King's court) and answer to the Justice Minister. However, the Diwan, not the Minister, has the power to remove judges. Jeddah's judicial complex is a court of first instance. The Kingdom's two appellate courts (engaged automatically in criminal cases, wherein they are referred to as the cassation courts) are located in Mecca and Riyadh, and the Supreme Judicial Council also resides in the capital. An independent grievance board is empowered to investigate allegations of judicial corruption and malfeasance. Ministries may, if requested by a party to a case and approved by the presiding judge, submit briefs on cases related to their areas of responsibility. According to Abu Rashed, such approval rarely is given, because judges in the Hejaz prize their independence and tend to suspect interested parties of seeking to unfairly influence outcomes.

On the afternoon of June 25, Abu Rashed and I attended *Sharia* court proceedings involving his client, a Saudi man, who was being sued by his Syrian-born wife for divorce. The couple had four children ranging in age from three months to five years and neither party was contesting the divorce action (which the wife filed on the grounds that her husband was never around). The issues the parties wanted the judge to consider were the divorce itself and custody of the children.

Abu Rashed explained to me how custody is adjudicated here. Per *Sharia*, children who are under age seven should reside with their mothers. After that, they are to reside with their fathers. Fathers are, at all times, obliged to support their children according to their means (as determined by the judge). The incarceration, illness, or mental incapacity of either parent can provide exceptions to the foregoing guidelines. In addition, if the divorced parents do not reside reasonably close to one another, then the father may (in the case of children under seven) argue that he should have custody in order to properly administer child support. According to Abu Rashed, his client—a resident of al-Baha (a governorate south of Mecca)—hoped to use this exception to persuade the judge that he should have custody of the children instead of his Jeddah-resident wife.

At about 1:30 p.m., the clerk of the court ushered Abu Rashed, a KAAU law student serving as Abu Rashed's clerk, the defendant, the plaintiff, the plaintiff's brother, and me into the spacious—if somewhat tatty—chamber of the judge, Shaykh Abd al-Rahman al-Hejailan (no relation to the famous attorney). Seated behind an office desk, the judge addressed the attendees, who were arrayed in three rows of chairs in front of his desk. Abu Rashed, his assistant, his client, and the plaintiff's brother (speaking on his sister's behalf) occupied the first row. I sat in the second row and the plaintiff sat in the third holding her infant daughter. The judge read the names of all present and instructed the clerk to write them in a large, clothbound ledger. He noted for the record that the suit had been filed by the plaintiff, whom he said merited equal treatment under the law even though she was a female born in Damascus. Next, he reviewed the facts of the case as presented by both parties. As these were not in dispute, he moved quickly on to the issue of divorce.

The judge spoke uninterrupted for several minutes about his philosophy and the requirements of *Sharia* pertaining to divorce. He said that he strongly preferred that the parties make every attempt to reconcile and asked the plaintiff and defendant whether they could try to do this. Through her brother, the plaintiff explained that she had tried for six months to convince her husband to live with her, but he refused. The husband, through Abu Rashed, did not deny this, but stated that he no longer loved his wife and wished to move on with his life. Both then asked about custody, at which point the judge cut them off, stating that he would decide that day the divorce question only; the matter of child custody would have to be the subject of another proceeding at a later date.

The judge asked the couple if it was their intention to divorce. The answer being in the affirmative, he directed the defendant to say aloud that he divorced his wife. Given the facts and the inability of the couple to reconcile, the judge continued, he was granting a divorce. However, he instructed the clerk to enter only one divorce in the ledger (three are required to permanently dissolve a marriage). If, after 40 days, both parties still wanted to go through with the divorce, then the defendant could return and pronounce his divorce in court twice (both utterances being recorded in the ledger) and it would be final.

In the meantime, implored the judge, both husband and wife must consider the consequences of their actions. He observed that the 40-day period should be used for reflection and reasoned thought about what was best for the children. He then ruled that the defendant should pay the plaintiff 10,000 riyals (about $2,667), the amount the wedding contract stipulated that the groom would give the bride in case of divorce (the contract having been entered as evidence during a previous proceeding). The nearly ex-husband readily agreed. With that, the judge dictated a case summary to the clerk, who laboriously wrote it in the ledger. Following handshakes all around, the group filed out of the chamber at approximately 2:30 p.m.

At lunch afterward, Abu Rashed explained that most divorce cases do not go so smoothly. Often, the parties become hostile and have to be kept physically separated. It is rare to see the plaintiff and the defendant agree with the judge and with each other on the facts. According to Abu Rashed, having a lawyer present usually results in more orderly proceedings. In this case, for instance, he was able to remind the judge about pertinent information and documents that bolstered both sides' claims of irreconcilable differences.

Saudi judges appreciate it when attorneys play a helpful role, continued Abu Rashed. Filing at the courts is hit-or-miss, he observed, with all information still handwritten and kept by the judges, not a central library. The result is that each jurist employs his own record-keeping system, making broad-based legal research a virtual impossibility. In response, law firms in the Hejaz keep their own files on cases in which they have been involved, complete with verbatim copies of what judges order to be entered in the ledgers. Increasingly, this practice has proved to be of real assistance in fostering a reliance on precedent in adjudicating cases. Abu Rashed said that when a lawyer is able to tell a judge that he made such-and-such a ruling in a similar case some years ago (when, in all probability, the judge would be unable to find the record of the prior case without expending considerable time and effort), it makes the court's job much easier and speeds the process along.

Finding ways to further accelerate the legal process was the stated goal of Mecca Governor Prince Abd al-Majeed during his meeting with the heads of the governorate's courts, also on June 25, 2000. According to Abu Rashed, the most common complaints registered with the grievance board are that the Saudi legal system is inefficient, loses documents, and moves too slowly. An item in the English-language Hejazi daily *Saudi Gazette* on June 26, 2000, state that Abd al-Majeed hoped his meeting would produce recommendations to upgrade the courts' performances so that they are able to "cope with the requirements of the time."

Abu Rashed told me that a computerization initiative at the administrative law court has met with great success, and that similar efforts were scheduled to begin in the labor and banking/financial courts that fall. The *Sharia* courts will be the last to undergo computerization, he averred, because the judges there are the most averse to change and because of the religious sensitivities inherent in switching from pens to pixels, the latter enjoying no clear analogous support in the Qur'an.

Debating Religious Freedom (March 2001)

A delegation from the U.S. Commission on International Religious Freedom (USCIRF) arrived in Jeddah from Riyadh on the afternoon of March 27, 2001. Led by USCIRF Chairman Elliott Abrams, the group's members included Dr. Laila al-Marayati, Cardinal Theodore McCarrick, USCIRF Executive Director Steven McFarland, Rabbi David Saperstein, and staff researcher Khaled Elgindy. The delegation met first with Islamic Affairs Minister Salih bin Abd al-Aziz Al al-Shaykh at his office near the U.S. Consulate General. Although the Minister understands and speaks some English, he used his deputy, Dr. Adnan al-Wazzan, to interpret.

Minister Al al-Shaykh declared that he welcomed the visitors in the spirit of dialogue and that he had "nothing to hide." No topics were off limits. He continued that Islam, as a global faith, was of necessity open to exchanges of ideas. Muslims, he observed, support diversity of cultures and peoples. That said, they cannot permit changes to the fundamental tenets of Islam. *Ijtihad*, or interpretation of doctrine, only is permissible in certain narrowly defined circumstances. Remarking that he did not want to rehash what the Commission members had heard from officials in the capital, the Minister said it was important to understand Saudi Arabia's unique role in Islam. The Kingdom, as the birthplace and center of the faith, bears a special responsibility toward Muslims everywhere.

Abrams thanked the Minister for receiving the delegation, introduced its members, and stated that they were there to learn more about the policy of permitting private worship by non-Muslims in the Kingdom while prohibiting them from taking part in public ceremonies. Where, he asked, is the line separating the two? Americans of other faiths residing in Saudi Arabia want to be sure to stay on the right side of the line.

Al al-Shaykh responded by noting the Qur'anic affirmation that there is no compulsion in religion and that, in Islamic countries such as Syria and Iraq, one can find churches standing next to mosques. But that is not possible in the Kingdom because of its special role in Islam. Thus, non-Muslims must worship privately, which means on their own property (in their home, office, and so on) and in small groups only. Pushed to elucidate further by Abrams and Cardinal McCarrick, the Minister defined private worship as that which does not perturb the neighbors. He also stated that a particular house should not be used by non-Muslims as a regular place of worship because that would be tantamount to the establishment of a church, something that was expressly forbidden by the Prophet who, according to a *hadith*, stated that the Arabian Peninsula could abide only the Islamic faith.

McCarrick asked Al al-Shaykh about the special case of Catholicism. As a Eucharistic faith, it requires priests. Could a priest come to Saudi Arabia, quietly and without a clerical collar, to celebrate mass? Could a priest enter the country as an engineer or a doctor and minister to Catholics on his own time? The Minister smiled and responded that this already occurs with no problems. He quoted the Arabic proverb that respect for others' feelings is part of human nature. He then said that although the United States and European nations permit the establishment of mosques, they generally do not allow them to broadcast the prayer call five times a day as is required in Islam. We do not protest this prohibition because we understand that it is based on laws that apply to everyone, Muslims and non-Muslims alike. Laws, he declaimed, reflect the desires of people living under them, and we respect them.

Al al-Shaykh compared the Arabian Peninsula to the Vatican. Obviously, he said, one is much large than the other, but both serve as special sanctuaries for their respective faiths. He then asked McCarrick whether Orthodox Christians are permitted to worship in the Vatican. The latter responded in the affirmative. Rabbi Saperstein chimed in that he had visited the Vatican and felt free to worship there as a Jew. McCarrick said that, to his knowledge, there are no Muslims living in Vatican City. However, if there were and if they wished to build a mosque there, he would support them. If you move there, he said to the Minister, we will build you a mosque. Al al-Shaykh laughingly replied that he would be ready to go next week.

Abrams returned to the subject of private versus public worship by non-Muslims in the Kingdom. If the difference depends on what the neighbors think, then it seems less a matter of law than an arbitrary standard. The Minister responded that, under *Sharia*, the feelings of the *umma* (community of believers) are part of the legal code. All Muslims are responsible for upholding the faith. Abrams rejoined with a hypothetical situation: If my two brothers and I and our families, totaling some 15 people, wish to get together once a week and worship in my home, how am I to know at what point we are in danger of attracting negative attention? Suppose we are quiet and discreet. If a neighbor nonetheless takes it upon himself to call the *mutawwa'in* (religious police), will I be punished? Al al-Shaykh replied that the non-Muslims in such a scenario would have nothing to fear. As long as they meet the standard of private, quiet worship, complaints by neighbors would be regarded as unjustified.

Picking up on the *mutawwa'in* thread, Dr. al-Marayati asked the Minister to explain how he reconciled the Qur'an's injunction against compulsion in religion with the activities of the religious police. Al al-Shaykh answered that the role of the *mutawwa'in* is to remind non-Muslims to respect the faith, not to tell people what to believe; it is a matter of respecting Muslims' feelings. Al-Marayati then raised the issue of the religious police's dealings with other Muslims. Do they not try to tell other Muslims how to behave? Is this not compulsion? The Minister replied by explaining that Islam is meant to prepare believers for the Day of Judgment and the Hereafter. The *mutawwa'in* help to remind Muslims to focus on the fact that their goal should be securing passage to Heaven, not an easy life in the here-and-now. The religious police, he said, administer "preventive medicine" to Muslims to keep them on the right path.

Saperstein presented Al al-Shaykh with another hypothetical situation involving the standard of reasonableness applied to non-Muslim worship in Saudi Arabia: Say you are friends with a Hindu family living next door. You know they invite people over from time to time to worship quietly. Another neighbor on your block objects to this, but you do not. That neighbor insists on calling the *mutawwa'in* to put a stop to the Hindus' worship. Should they be arrested? The Minister replied that no, they absolutely should not be arrested. The Hindus clearly are abiding by what any Muslim would regard to be a reasonable standard of quiet worship and so should not be molested in any way. Asked by Saperstein to whom complaints should be addressed if non-Muslims praying privately in their homes experience an incursion by the authorities, Al al-Shaykh said that he would receive them.

Saperstein thanked the Minister for identifying how reasonableness enters into the equation and asked whether he, somehow, could lead an effort to better inform Saudis about this standard. Al al-Shaykh said that this already is codified in the Kingdom's contract law, wherein employers are told they must give non-Muslim employees private time for worship, but added that it is difficult to fault believers for being overly zealous in defending their faith. The USCIRF delegation members thanked the Minister for his hospitality and forthrightness and the meeting concluded.

The delegation next met with Prince Abd al-Aziz bin Fahd, the Council of Ministers president and the King's youngest son, at Al-Salaam Palace on the Jeddah corniche. He received the members in an opulent salon overlooking the Red Sea and, speaking through Adel al-Jubayr (a 30-something, fluent English-speaking Foreign Ministry official who recently returned from an assignment at the Saudi Embassy in Washington and now serving as Crown Prince Abdallah's foreign affairs adviser), welcomed them in his father's name to Saudi Arabia. The 30-year-old Abd al-Aziz said the visitors should regard the Kingdom as their "second country" because of the special relationship it has enjoyed with the United States since the 1945 meeting between President Franklin Roosevelt and Ibn Saud aboard the USS Quincy. This friendship has remained strong because both sides, he insisted, recognize the value of dialogue.

Prince Abd al-Aziz continued that the Saudi-U.S. relationship is more than merely a government-to-government phenomenon. The people of both nations have enjoyed exchanges and continue to work toward understanding one another better. He added that he welcomed the opportunity to discuss religious freedom issues with the USCIRF delegation.

Chairman Abrams thanked the prince for receiving the group and said that he would, owing to the short time available, live up to an unfortunate stereotype of Americans and move directly into substance: We are trying, he said, to understand better the practice of religious freedom in Saudi Arabia, both for non-Muslims and for non-Wahhabi Muslims. We would like to know your perspective on the limits.

Prince Abd al-Aziz replied that he viewed persecution of any human being, for any reason, as abhorrent. This is not something any government should do. The Kingdom is completely opposed to this. He went on to note that both the United States and Saudi Arabia believe that a government's primary function is to care for its citizens. All Saudi citizens are Muslims, and they were so before the establishment of the third Saudi state 100 years ago.[3] The Prince repeated the Vatican analogy used by the Islamic Affairs Minister and added that he hoped the delegation members would, the next time they visited the Kingdom, be able to travel about the countryside. There, he said, they would encounter the real Saudi Arabia and see the essential conservatism of its people. It is with these citizens' sensitivities in mind that the government has enforced the prohibition on public religious services by anyone other than Muslims.

Cardinal McCarrick stated that he appreciated the Kingdom's role as a special place in the heart of Muslims akin to the Vatican's position among Catholics. He emphasized that it would be ideal for the delegation's discussions to lead to some sort of ongoing dialogue. For instance, he said, regular meetings between Vatican and Saudi religious officials would serve to bolster mutual understanding, a boon for both sides.

The Prince said he agreed and quoted a Qur'anic verse stating that "the closest of the faiths to Islam is Christianity." He recalled that there had been an active and ongoing dialogue between the Kingdom and the Catholic church during the 1970s and 1980s and remarked that it would be good to reestablish this exchange. Prince Abd al-Aziz then said that he had an important point to make: Rather than beginning dialogue at the ground level, both sides should focus on their mutual goals and objectives. In other words, he explained, it would be more productive to work toward shared ideals of building better and more tolerant human beings than on disputing where mosques and churches can and cannot be built. He added that history should be seen as a guide. Excessive emphasis on the status of holy places had led to, among other tragedies, the Crusades. In this day of the global village, it is a crime that we have not made a greater effort to understand one another better. The prince concluded by declaring that Christians and Muslims must unite to work for the benefit of humanity.

Chairman Abrams told Prince Abd al-Aziz that the delegation had the impression that there are large numbers of non-Muslims in the Kingdom who are unable to practice their religions. He noted that Christians are imperiled if they gather in anything but small numbers for worship and that Shia face job discrimination and cannot build their own mosques. How could the prince, as a man of faith, abide such things if the ultimate objective is to make better human beings by allowing them to worship God?

The prince responded that he did not believe that any Saudi would threaten non-Muslims or Shia. The Qur'an explicitly forbids forced conversions and stipulates the protection of non-Muslims. With regard to the Shia, the Saudi Ambassador to Iran is a Shia. There are five or six other ambassadors who are Shia. Several members of the Consultative Council are Shia and there have been Shia ministers in the past. The King enjoys close friendships with a number of Shia. Shia do have their own places of worship and no one interferes with them. Where there are restrictions, these are based not on faith but on security considerations. A Shia imam can preach what he wants, but he may not incite sectarianism. Sunni imams work under the same prohibition. Before the Al Saud unified the Kingdom, sectarianism had rendered the Arabian

Peninsula a lawless place. Nowadays, people live securely and respect each other. We aim, he said, to keep the peace.

Prince Abd al-Aziz wrapped up the meeting with a soliloquy comparing Saudi Arabia to other Muslim states and the West. He said that although there may be individuals in the Kingdom who transgress against the law, this is not state policy. It is like the Los Angeles Police Department: You cannot blame the entire institution for the actions of one or two bad people. Similarly, when one examines how citizens are treated in other Muslim states, Saudi Arabia looks good. That is not to say there are no problems here; the Kingdom remains a developing country and there is room for improvement. Europe endured 300 years of sectarian warfare before finally achieving some semblance of a lasting peace. Saudi Arabia has been around only for 100 years, but, he said, we think what we have achieved is impressive when you put it into context.

A Matter of Interpretation (April 2001)

We have attempted to explain the Saudi prohibition on non-Muslim houses of worship in the Kingdom. Those who engage Saudi government and religious figures on this point invariably meet with the same response: Saudi Arabia, indeed, the entire Arabian Peninsula is the "Vatican of Islam." The Prophet, on his deathbed, told his followers that there should be only one religion here. Pressed to explain where this comes from, our interlocutors say it is a *hadith*, a verified narrative describing the words of or example set by Muhammad, and therefore a matter of faith.

Hadith come in varying degrees of reliability depending on their provenance and chain of transmitters. The shorter the chain and the more esteemed the people who comprise it, the better the *hadith*. There are four schools of (Sunni) Islamic jurisprudence: Hanafi, Maliki, Shaf'i, and Hanbali. Each favors different compilations of the *hadith*.[4]

For most Saudis, the *Sahih al-Bukhari* and the *Sahih al-Muslim* (*sahih* meaning, roughly, authentications) are the most authoritative compilations of *hadith*. However, some also refer to others, such as the *Muwatta of Imam Malik ibn Anas*, the compilation used by the oldest school of Islamic jurisprudence, the Maliki. Because Malik's *Muwatta* was the first compilation, many of its *hadith* have the shortest (and thus, for Malikis at least, the most reliable) transmission chains.

The *hadith* in which Muhammad declares the Arabian Peninsula to be an Islam-only zone appears twice each in Malik's *Muwatta*, the

Sahih al-Muslim and the *Sahih al-Bukhari*. Malik's versions are the least frequently quoted. Following is the first appearance:

Yahya related to me from Malik from Ismail ibn Abi Hakim that he heard Omar ibn Abd al-Aziz say, "One of the last things the Messenger of God, may God bless him and grant him peace, said was, 'May God fight the Jews and the Christians. They took the graves of their prophets as places of prostration. Two religions shall not coexist in the land of the Arabs.'"

Following is the second ibn Malik citation:

Yahya related to me from Malik from ibn Shihab that the Messenger of God, may God bless him and grant him peace, said, "Two religions shall not coexist in the Arabian Peninsula." Malik said that ibn Shihab said, "Omar ibn al-Khattab searched for information about that until he was absolutely convinced that the Messenger of God, may God bless him and grant him peace, had said, 'Two religions shall not coexist in the Arabian Peninsula,' and he therefore expelled the Jews from Khaybar.'"[5]

Al-Muslim's versions, identical except that one is narrated by Omar ibn al-Khattab and the other by Said bin Jubayr, are the most straightforward. They appear as follows:

It has been narrated by Omar ibn al-Khattab (Said bin Jubayr) that he heard the Messenger of God, may God bless him and grant him peace, say, "I will expel the Jews and Christians from the Arabian Peninsula and will not leave any but a Muslim."

Al -Bukhari's two versions are the most emotional and, perhaps for this reason, the most popular among Saudis. The first version follows:

Ibn Abbas said, "Thursday! What (great thing) took place on Thursday!" Then he started weeping until his tears wet the gravel on the ground. Then he said, "On Thursday the illness of God's Messenger was aggravated and he said, 'Fetch me writing materials so that I may have something written to you after which you will never go astray.' The people (present there) differed in this matter and people should not differ before a prophet. They said, 'God's Messenger is seriously ill.' The Prophet said, 'Let me alone, for the state in which I am now is better that what you are calling me for.' The Prophet on his deathbed gave three orders, saying, 'Expel the pagans from the Arabian Peninsula, respect and give gifts to the foreign delegates as you have seen me dealing with them.' I forgot the third (order)." Yaqub bin Muhammad said, "I asked al-Mughira bin Abd al-Rahman about the Arabian Peninsula, and he said, 'It comprises Mecca, Medina, al-Yamama, and Yemen.' Yaqub added, 'And al-Arj, the beginning of Tihama.'"

The second al-Bukhari version reads as follows:

Narrated Said bin Jubayr that he heard ibn Anas saying, "Thursday! And you know not what Thursday is?" After that ibn Anas wept until the stones on the ground were soaked with his tears. On that I asked ibn Anas, "What is Thursday?" He said, "When the condition of God's Messenger deteriorated, he said, 'Bring me a bone of scapula, so that I may write something for you after which you will never go astray.' The people differed in their opinions although it was improper to differ in front of a prophet. They said, 'What is wrong with him? Do you think he is delirious? Ask him (to find out).' The Prophet replied, 'Leave me as I am in a better state than what you are asking me to do.' Then the Prophet ordered them to do three things, saying, 'Turn out all the pagans from the Arabian Peninsula, show respect to all foreign delegates by giving them gifts as I used to do.' The sub-narrator added, "The third order was something beneficial which either ibn Anas did not mention or he mentioned but I forgot."

To underscore what they believe to be the superiority of their faith, Saudis frequently will point out that the Qur'an, unlike the Torah and the Bible, embodies the immutable, literal word of God. It appears today, they insist, as it divinely was dictated to Muhammad more than 14 centuries ago. No human has corrupted it by changing one word, a major reason why most Muslims regard translations of the Arabic original into other tongues as imperfect if not sacrilegious.

The *hadith*, on the other hand, manifestly are the work and words of humans. A huge amount of effort has been expended by generations of Muslims authenticating the provenance of individual citations and placing them within the correct context. Moreover, unlike the Qur'an for which only one version of the text exists, there are several different compilations of the *hadith* and sometimes variant versions of the same *hadith* within a single compilation.

In examining the *hadith* used to justify excluding non-Muslim houses of worship in the Kingdom, a number of questions arise: Did Muhammad really intend to expel Christians and Jews—and not merely "pagans"—from the Arabian Peninsula? Was the Prophet in his right mind when he made this utterance? Precisely what geographic entities are meant by the "Arabian Peninsula" and the "land of the Arabs?" In one of the Maliki and one of the al-Muslim versions, Omar ibn al-Khattab, the second caliph, is a key transmitter. It was under his rule that Christians and Jews who did not embrace Islam were forcibly ejected from Arabia, and Wahhabis esteem him as the best of the four "rightly guided" caliphs who succeeded Muhammad and presided over the putative golden age of early Islam. Did he put words into Muhammad's mouth to justify his actions?

Whisperers (October 2001)

The Qur'an, in verses 26–27 of *surah* 15 ("The Valley of Stone"), states that before God created humans out of "an altered black mud" he had brought forth *jinn*, beings made of "smokeless fire."[6] *Jinn* are an integral part of both traditional and Gnostic Islamic belief. They are referred to 25 times in the Qur'an, not counting *surah* 72 ("The Jinn"). The holy book's first *surah*, called "Al-Fatiha" (the opening), generally is regarded as equivalent to the Christian profession of faith. In it, believers acknowledge that "all praise is due to God, Lord of the worlds." Some Muslim scholars theorize that the physical plane humans inhabit is only one of five coexisting worlds or "divine presences," seen and unseen, governed by God. Meanwhile, the degrees of being separating creation from the creator are spoken of in the Qur'an symbolically as seven spheres or heavens, the last of which is the furthest from the material world and the closest to God (hence the term "seventh heaven").

Humans and *jinn* occupy different dimensions of the same sphere, while angels reside beyond the spheres in paradise. Some theologians have postulated the existence of other beings in between. However, Muslims believe only God has knowledge of all the worlds and the full extent of his creation. Because of their limited understanding, the *jinn* and mankind must rely on faith to arrive at any conception of the realms beyond their perception.

The Arabic word *jinn* is derived from the verb *janna*, which means to hide or conceal, and it is a tenet of traditional Islamic faith that every human being has a *qareen* or invisible *jinn* counterpart. This lifelong companion appeals to one's carnal desires and tries to divert him or her from the path of righteousness, and it is this being whom a Muslim addresses when—upon completing supplications—he or she whispers "may the peace and mercy of God be upon you" over each shoulder. *Jinn* marry, have children, practice a variety of religions (including Islam), and eventually die. They live far longer than mere mortals, however, and a few clerics speculate that there are *jinn* today who were alive during the time of the Prophet Muhammad. Like humans, *jinn* are endowed with the capacity to distinguish between good and evil and will be called on the Day of Judgment to account for their lives before God. The *jinn*'s purpose in life is precisely the same as that of humans. As the Qur'an quotes God in *surah* 51 ("The Scattering Winds") verse 56, "I did not create the *jinn* and mankind except to worship me."

Sufis and other practitioners of Gnostic Islam believe there are some visible *jinn*, ascribing to them various moral and physical qualities. *Jinn* who live among humans are called *amaar* and those that antagonize the young are termed *arwaah*. Evil *jinn* are *shayateen* (the plural form of *shaytan* or satan) and, if they become powerful, are called *afreet*. Some *jinn* are beautiful, while others—especially the *afreet* and the *ghul* (from which our word ghoul derives)—are hideous. According to the *Mushkil al-Athaar* and the *Al-Kabir*, two compilations of *hadith* (narrations of the Prophet's deeds and utterances as recounted by his companions) used by Hejazi Sufis, some *jinn* have wings and fly while others resemble snakes and dogs. A third type can masquerade as or possess human beings. According to a more widely accepted *hadith* compilation, the *Al-Muwatta of Ibn Malik*, Muhammad warned his followers that "there are *jinn* in Medina who have become Muslims. When you see one of them, call out to it for three days. If it appears after that, then kill it, for it is a *shaytan*."

Many Muslims accept that *jinn*, in addition to their invisibility, are endowed with the ability to transport themselves and objects great distances with incredible speed. Islam also credits the *jinn* with a limited capacity for prognostication, in that their lightning-fast transits between the physical and immaterial worlds enable them to perceive unfolding events sooner than can mere mortals. Magicians thus are disapproved of within Islam as people who commune with the *jinn*, sometimes to the point that they sell their own souls in exchange for the *jinn* making them appear to have extraordinary knowledge or powers. Fortunetellers also are deemed dangerous in that they are able to manipulate a "client" by conspiring with his or her *qareen*. According to several *hadith*, the Prophet advised Muslims to stay away from such people: "The prayer of one who approaches a fortuneteller and asks him about anything will not be accepted for 40 days or nights," and "Whosoever approaches a fortuneteller and believes in what he says has disbelieved in what was revealed to Muhammad."

Jinn hardly require human assistance to trick mankind, however. Islamic scholars point out that, by posing as prophets and by "possessing" idols, *jinn* have from time immemorial sought to foster polytheism, a trend they believe was arrested in the Arabs' case by the appearance of Muhammad. Of course, not only the Arabs are potentially susceptible to this kind of deception. Many Hejazis believe that the modern West's apparent preoccupation with flying saucers and aliens, visions of saints, séances, witchcraft, and ghosts signals a woeful ignorance of the fact that all such phenomena are explained by the powers and abilities of the *jinn*. Accordingly, only by embracing and practicing Islam can a person acquire sufficient understanding to defend against the *jinn* lying in wait to trip one up. As the Qur'an states in *surah* 7 ("The Elevations") verse 27, "Indeed he (Iblis) and his tribe watch you from a position where you cannot seem them."[7]

All mortals have encounters, consciously or not, with *jinn*, but the Qur'an highlights the interactions of the *jinn* with the prophets Sulayman (Solomon) and Muhammad. *Surah* 38 ("Sa'd," a letter of the Arabic alphabet) explains why God nullified the covenants he had made with King David and the Israelites and replaced them with a compact promising grace and salvation to all believers, not just to a chosen people. Amid a narration describing the special privileges once afforded the House of David, verses 35–39 assert that God had placed the *jinn* under Sulayman's command so that he might build the temple and humble the Queen of Saba (Sheba). The point is amplified in *surahs* 34 and 27 ("Sheba" and "The Ants," respectively). The latter, in verse 17, states that "gathered for Sulayman were his soldiers of the *jinn* and men and birds, and they were (marching) in rows."

References to Muhammad's interactions with the *jinn* are peppered throughout the Qur'an, but it is in *surah* 72 ("The Jinn") that his relationship with them is most fully explored. The story goes that, on his way to Ta'if from Mecca, the Prophet recited the Qur'an at night in the desert. A party of *jinn* came to listen and were convinced of Islam's validity. They returned later with their chiefs who—upon hearing the sacred verses—embraced the new faith and swore an oath of allegiance to Muhammad. The spot where this event occurred is today surrounded by a cemetery at the intersection of al-Majeed al-Haram and al-Juhfah streets in northern Mecca. It is marked by a small house of worship known as the al-Jinn Mosque, which reputedly is several hundred years old.

Muslims' belief in unseen, possibly malicious "others" bespeaks neither irrationality nor a particular cultural eccentricity. Spirits play prominent roles in many other faiths, including—and perhaps especially—Christianity. In Book Eight of his seminal work *The City of God* (circa 400), St. Augustine of Hippo accepts the existence of supernatural beings in refuting the proposition of the neo-Platonist philosopher and rhetorician Apuleius that demons should be worshipped as messengers and mediators between gods and men. Augustine argues it is impossible for humans to be reconciled to "good gods" by demons, who are the slaves of vice and who delight in "that which good and wise men abhor and condemn"—namely, poetry, theater, and magic.

Some later Christians also have acknowledged that the world holds ample room for mystery. In *Paradise Lost* (1667), the English poet John Milton wrote that "millions of spiritual beings unseen walk the earth up and down." According to Ralph Waldo Emerson, "God himself does not speak prose, but communicates with us by hints, omens, inferences and dark resemblances in objects lying all around us" (1872).[8] Even Ronald Reagan alluded to reason's inability to account completely for reality as we know it when he said, "God's miracles are to be found in nature itself; the wind and waves, the wood that becomes a tree—all of these are explained biologically, but behind them is the hand of God. And I believe that is true of creation itself" (1976).[9]

Muslims' conception of the *jinn* would be of merely academic interest were it not for the fact that some here believe the Saudis accused of participating in the terrorist attacks of September 11 either were not really there or—if they were—were not acting of their own free will. A surprising number of highly educated Hejazis insist that *jinn* stole the identities of or possessed the hijackers; a few even claim Usama Bin Ladin himself must be a *shaytan* or an *afreet* to successfully have convinced the young Saudis to annihilate themselves and so many others. Amid the torrent of rumors and misinformation swirling among residents in the Hejaz, there have been a few calls for Muslim introspection. Several local imams have been noted as referring believers to *surah* 114 ("Mankind") of the Qur'an, which reads, "I seek refuge in the Lord of mankind, the Sovereign of mankind, the God of mankind, from the evil of the retreating whisperer—who whispers evil into the breasts of mankind from among the *jinn* and mankind."

The Hejazi Origins of Wahhabi Intolerance (April 2002)[10]

Considerable attention has been directed at Wahhabism in recent months. Journalists, scholars, and policymakers have asked what about the puritanical creed impelled 15 young Saudis (most of whom were from the western and southern parts of the Kingdom) to cast their lot with Usama Bin Ladin and participate in the attacks of September 11. Some have looked back to the unforgiving realities of eighteenth-century Najd (the milieu that spawned the sect's founder, Muhammad ibn Abd al-Wahhab) for answers. Others have indicted the brutal excesses of the Taliban, the *uber*-Wahhabis of our day, while studying the spread of this particular brand of extremism. In the course of these examinations, many have cited Saudi Arabia's refusal to play host to non-Muslim houses of worship as the very embodiment of religious bigotry. Nearly all have decried the apparent misogyny behind the religious establishment's continued insistence on depriving Saudi women of the mobility and autonomy their sisters in neighboring states take for granted.

Wahhabism's intolerance derives from its adherents' insistence that not only does Islam have a monopoly on divine truth, but that its sole legitimate form is based on a narrow, literal reading of the Qur'an and the *hadith*. All other interpretations are regarded as innovations likely to lead Muslims into polytheism. Fear of deviating from the correct faith, combined with an evangelical zeal to keep others on the straight path, drives Wahhabis toward uncompromising, doctrinaire positions. They maintain these positions by harking back to Islam's formative years in the land of its birth, the Hejaz.[11]

Conventional Muslim, and especially Wahhabi, wisdom holds that the *jahaliyya*, or age of ignorance, prevailed before the coming of Islam. Seventh-century Hejazis—heirs to the tradition of Ibrahim (Abraham) through his eldest son, Ismail (Ishmael)—are said to have forgotten the imperative of worshipping the One God. Owing to the unchecked innovations that polluted their formerly pure faith, they were reduced to living as immoral pagans who treated their women as chattel, committed infanticide, and warred constantly with one another. Because Mecca and other major Hejazi cities were on or near important overland trade routes, locals were exposed to the religious traditions of South Arabia, Mesopotamia, Egypt, and the Byzantine and Sassanid (Persian) empires. Elements of Zoroastrianism, Manichaeism, Monophysitism, and Talmudism, as well as various astral cults and animist traditions, infused and further confused beliefs.

Muslim tradition further holds that the Prophet Muhammad, member of the Bani Hashim clan of Mecca's dominant Quraysh tribe, rose to prominence by preaching a clear, unambiguous message calling on Arabs to return to absolute monotheism. An upright man regarded as a *hanif*, or self-styled professor of the Ibrahimic belief system, Muhammad was chosen to receive the ultimate divine revelations (later compiled into the Qur'an) explicitly instructing mankind on how to live in accordance with God's will. Although his message was at first rejected, it came to be embraced by the Hejazis. After subduing the Jews of Medina and making it the first Muslim city, Muhammad marched triumphantly into Mecca to destroy the idols that crowded the Kaaba, the original house of worship rebuilt by Ibrahim. The new faith spread rapidly to Damascus, Baghdad, and beyond. Islam, the total submission to God, liberated Arabs (and others) from the shackles of superstition and idolatry.

The reality of pre-Islamic Arabia was more complex. Some seventh-century Hejazis were pagans, but many were not. Aside from a goodly number of Christians and Jews, Mecca was home to a flourishing moon goddess cult that served as the "official" faith of the Quraysh. Being savvy businesspeople (women—including Muhammad's first wife, Khadija—were prominent merchants in those days), the Quraysh allowed many other faiths to worship at the Kaaba and even went so far as to install within it 360 pictures and idols, including Jewish and Christian symbols, contributed by various tribes.[12] Mecca, roughly the halfway point along the western incense route from Dhofar and Hadhramaut to the Levant, became such a popular stopping point for caravans that other cities—notably Sanaa and Najran—attempted to duplicate its successful formula of *laissez-faire* trade combined with religious tolerance. None came close to challenging Mecca's preeminence.

Muhammad at first was treated as just another harmless local cult leader by Mecca's leaders. His god, Allah, belonged to the local pantheon as the imageless "father" of al-Lat, their threefold moon goddess (al-Lat, al-Uzza, and Manat).[13] However, many Meccans owed their wealth to the city's numerous religious festivals, especially the annual hajj, which began centuries earlier as a celebration of the rains that marked summer's end. They were alarmed by the Prophet's growing popularity and vocal insistence that all the idols worshipped at the Kaaba (including the Nabatean god Hubal, a gold-bedecked, carnelian statue of a man affixed to the top of the structure and posited as its protector) were blasphemous and had to be destroyed. In classic Hejazi fashion, the Quraysh elders attempted to co-opt him by proposing a deal: Endorse our highly profitable pantheistic enterprise and we will ensure preferential access for you and your followers to all the festivities.

Muhammad nearly was taken in. He announced having received new revelations, including the following verse:

"Have you then considered al-Lat and al-Uzza, and Manat, the third, the other? These are the exalted birds whose intercession is approved." Stunned by their leader's apparent compromise, many of the Prophet's faithful threatened to abandon him, causing him to repudiate the so-called "satanic verses." The lines were revised as follows: "Have you considered al-Lat and al-Uzza, and Manat, the third, the other? Are yours the males and his the females? That indeed were an unfair division! They are but names which you have named, you and your fathers, for which God has revealed no warrant. They follow but a guess and that which they themselves desire" (*surah* 53, verse 19).

As if not satisfied, Muhammad then delivered another divine dictate denying the existence of female angels:

"And how many angels are in the heavens whose intercession avails nothing save after God gives leave to whom he chooses and accepts! Most surely they who do not believe in the hereafter name the angels with female names" (*surah* 53, verse 26).

Sealing his fate, the Prophet then recited the infamous "verse of rejection" found in *surah* 109:

"Say: O disbelievers! I worship not that which you worship; nor worship you that which I worship. And I shall not worship that which you worship. Nor will you worship that which I worship. Unto you your religion, and unto me my religion."

The furious Quraysh put a price on Muhammad's head. Some of his followers found refuge in Christian Abyssinia, while the Messenger of God and a few stalwart companions (73 men and 3 women) undertook the flight (known as the *hijra*, the starting point of the Muslim calendar) to Medina. The Prophet's efforts to topple the moon goddess and rid Mecca of polytheism had begun in earnest.

Eight years after leaving Mecca in disgrace, Muhammad—who won power in Medina by mediating an end to a long-standing civil war and by subduing its rebellious tribes (including the Jews, who initially supported the Muslims)—returned as its conqueror. His first action was to cleanse the Kaaba. He ordered the destruction of all the pictures and idols (although legend has it that he spared a crucifix and portraits of Jesus and Mary), with he and his followers reciting "the truth has come, and falsehood has vanished" as they purged the structure. Black smoke, representing psychic influences, supposedly issued from some of the demolished deities. Hubal was stripped of his finery and turned into a doorstep. A new myth was fashioned for the black stone, forever divorcing it from the worship of al-Lat.

The moon goddess's priests and priestesses at the Kaaba, as well as those who attended her other shrines, either accepted Islam at swordpoint or were killed. According to *The Concise Encyclopaedia of Islam* (1999), the Prophet dispatched Khalid ibn Waleed, a converted Qurayshi who became a general in the Muslim army, to destroy the Mighty's temple at Nakhal. When he returned, the Prophet asked him whether he had seen anything. He replied in the negative. Muhammad stated, "You have not destroyed her," and ordered Khalid to return to Nakhal. This time, at the ruins of the temple, he saw a nude woman emerge, black with long, wild hair. As he slew her, he reportedly declaimed, "Al-Uzza, denial is for you, not worship." Similarly, Muslim forces commanded by the Prophet's companion Jarir ibn Abdallah were dispatched to al-Waliyyah to level the Dhu al-Khalasah. Vastly outnumbered, the men of the Banu Umamah and other tribes who attempted to defend the shrine were slaughtered and their women raped and enslaved along with their children. According to a *hadith*,

Muhammad is said to have commented, "This world shall not end until the buttocks of the women of Daws (again) wiggle around the Dhu al-Khalasah and they worship it as they were wont to do."

Mecca and Medina were the focal points of what Wahhabis regard as Islam's golden era, the period during which the community was presided over by the first four "rightly guided" caliphs. The history of that time is one of consolidation of authority, as well as initial attempts to standardize Muslim beliefs and practices according to the *sunna* (or traditions) of the Prophet (an effort that culminated in the compilation of the Qur'an). However, this time also witnessed the beginnings of the theological and ideological disputes that eventually would erupt and divide the Sunnis (followers of the *sunna* who believed the caliph should be determined by consensus, not heredity) from those who considered themselves partisans (*Shia*) of the fourth caliph, Muhammad's son-in-law, Ali. Revulsion at the "perversions" introduced by the Shia motivated some traditionalists to attempt to co-opt and to persecute the partisans' various minority sects. This, in turn, prompted the Shia to mount ever-more-extreme attempts to wrest control of the caliphate before ultimately ignoring it altogether.

As Islam's center of gravity shifted through the ensuing centuries to the Damascus of the Umayyads, the Baghdad of the Abbasids, the Cairo of the Fatimids, and the Istanbul of the Ottomans, the Hejaz devolved into a religious and cultural backwater. Ruled from afar by the Turks beginning in 966, the region was administered by a procession of *sharifs* (descendants of the Prophet through his grandson, Hassan) until 1925, when the last of these—Ali ibn Husayn ibn Ali al-Hashemi, later to be installed by the British as king in Iraq—was defeated by Ibn Saud. The "pure," uncompromising brand of Islam glorified by Muhammad ibn Abd al-Wahhab's Najdi enthusiasts had long since disappeared from the Holy Cities.[14] Their residents, perhaps dimly recalling the confessional comity that once characterized the Hejaz, readily accepted heterodox beliefs and practices. Tolerance had proven lucrative for a people who survived largely on revenues derived from the hajj trade.[15]

The Saudis did away with the Hashemites' corrupt, pilgrim-fleecing practices, earning them grudging respect from some Hejazis as well as the gratitude of pilgrims from throughout the Muslim world. For most, life in Mecca and Medina remained much as it had been until the 1930s and 1940s, when a world once again at war convinced King Abd al-Aziz that a national culture was needed to more firmly bind the disparate regions of his Arabian empire. Wahhabi overlords, who heretofore were restrained in the contempt with which they viewed the locals, were emboldened to insist that their ways were superior to indigenous practices. Since that time, zealots in and around the holy cities—many of them locals steeped in Wahhabi doctrine—have viewed themselves as free to continue the Prophet Muhammad's struggle to uproot and destroy all vestiges of the Hejaz's polytheistic past. The 1950s witnessed the replacement of all non-Saudi Islamic court justices with Najdis. The *mimbars* (pulpits) representing the four schools of (Sunni) Islamic jurisprudence were eliminated from the Grand Mosque in the 1960s. Numerous sites in the Hejaz revered by non-Wahhabis, including the homes and graves of holy personages (the Prophet's home in Mecca and the "tomb of Eve" in Jeddah among them), were bulldozed or paved over during the course of various mosque expansion and urban modernization projects in the 1970s.

In the wake of the Iranian Revolution and the takeover of the Grand Mosque in 1979 by self-styled Saudi *mahdi* Juhayman al-Utaybi and his fanatic millennialist followers (1979 corresponded to the Islamic year 1400), the Al Saud attempted to buy off domestic Sunni extremists by giving them more control over Saudi social life. The Kingdom's education and cultural ministries became centers of virulent Wahhabism, leading to the propagation of this exclusionary, hostile form of Islam both within and beyond the Kingdom's borders—with predictably disastrous results. Non-Saudi women, who never before had to wear the *abaya* (full-length black cloak) in the Hejaz, were compelled to cover up. Movie theaters (there were at least two operating in Jeddah until the early 1980s) were closed and greater restrictions placed on western Saudi Arabia's Muslim minorities, in particular the Shia in Medina and the Ismailis in Najran.[16] Nevertheless, the region's enduring, trade-driven tolerance may be what enabled it to escape the political violence witnessed elsewhere (for example, the Office of Program Management/Saudi Arabian National Guard (OPM/SANG) bombing in Riyadh and the al-Khobar Towers bombing in the Eastern Province) in the Kingdom in the 1990s.

Because the particulars of Islam's least liberal creed purport to draw on the faith's formative years in the holy cities, Hejazis—try as they might—cannot credibly characterize Wahhabism as a freak sectarian aberration. The Najdis' intolerant message succeeds because it remains unchallenged; no Muslim Luther has summoned the courage to nail his propositions to the door of the Kaaba. There are those who express hope that Islam, drawing on centuries of experience absorbing and, ultimately, de-fanging its radical fringe can harness the Wahhabis' drive and apply it to constructive purposes. It appears equally likely, however, that the as-yet-unchecked spread of Saudi Arabia's state faith could precipitate a cultural convulsion such as that which engulfed the West in the sixteenth century and subsequently was termed the Protestant Reformation. Then, Christendom struggled to amend itself while parrying perceived Muslim predations. Five hundred years later the tables are turned, and it is by no means clear whether Islam will accommodate itself to the emergence of a secular society or withdraw further into obscurantism and intolerance.

CHAPTER 5
Hinterlands

When you travel, remember that a foreign country is not designed to make you comfortable. It is designed to make its own people comfortable.
—Clifton Fadiman

Only two generations removed from a primitive existence little changed since antiquity, few Saudis know their country well. Sedentary Hejazis and their settled brethren elsewhere on the Arabian Peninsula rarely ventured far from the towns and villages. Those who did were traders, pilgrims, misfits, or some combination of the three. Leaving home was a perilous enterprise: The countryside and desert tracts were harsh and inhospitable and teemed with hostile, nomadic tribes. Pastoral pursuits ostensibly provided for the latters' survival, but their welfare also depended significantly on periodic raids on one another's camps and, more lucratively, upon the city folk. Caravans plying the spice routes were frequent and rich targets, ones that—for the right price—could be allowed to pass unmolested. Individual wanderers and outcasts rarely possessed the resources necessary to purchase such protection and, as a result, their journeys generally met with violent ends. Small wonder, then, that the idea of leisure travel within the Kingdom to this day retains the taint of trespass and appeals only to those who lack the means to vacation abroad.

Saudi Arabian Airlines and highways plied by long-distance bus services today connect the principal cities of the Kingdom. Jeddawis,

particularly those descended from Najdi carpetbaggers or employed by
the government or by businesses with head offices in the capital, regularly fly to Riyadh.[1] Ultraconservative citizens from Qassim and other
arid interior provinces like to unwind in the cool mountains of the
South. Southerners head for the Hejaz in search of jobs, Meccans in
search of open space trek the Ta'if highlands, and seasonal festivals
in Jeddah and elsewhere attract a trickle of travelers. But the idea of
exploring the length and breadth of Saudi Arabia for its own sake, of
hopping in the family car and lighting out for remote parts simply to see
and experience their country remains an alien concept to most Saudis.

At first glance, there is not much to recommend wandering off the
beaten track in Saudi Arabia. Seemingly interminable stretches of desolate dunes, parched prairies, and forbidding fields of stone greet the eye
without hinting that there is anything out there worth seeing. But worth-
while sites abound. The Kingdom is far more diverse, geologically and
sociologically, than one might imagine. Fragments of history and culture repose in the open, and encountering them requires only patience
and a little luck. Neolithic monuments lie scattered throughout the bleak
countryside, surrounded by the tools their builders dropped eons ago.
The many caves that pockmark the hills lining dry riverbeds hold pottery
shards and, sometimes, human remains. The Peninsula's savannah-like
past is depicted in rock-art galleries featuring long-gone fauna such as
elephants, giraffes, ostriches, impalas, and cheetahs. Troops of very-
much-alive baboons guard lichen-encrusted mountain passes with
carved steps, tributes to forgotten deities, and prayers chiseled in extinct
tongues. Representations of Ahura Mazda, the Zoroastrian sun god,
abound on boulders surrounding ancient pastures, and striking drawings
of spear-wielding hunters—some on horseback—leap from chasm walls
descending into deep, verdant valleys. Isolated wells and springs continue to provide life to villages as they have for millennia.

Few of these sites have been made public, let alone formally excavated.
Locals who know of them are reluctant to reveal their existence to outsiders, fearing both the invasion of their privacy and the unwelcome
attention of the Saudi authorities, who are quick to fence off and deny
access to lands deemed to have historic value. Indeed, it is ironic that,
although Wahhabi doctrine eschews the study of pre-Islamic life in
Arabia as tantamount to heresy, Riyadh has shown itself to act with surprising alacrity whenever an archeological find comes to light. Although
officials insist they act to protect antiquities from looters—a rationale not
difficult to defend given the citizenry's general disinterest in acknowledging, let alone preserving, the past—the biggest plunderer of all has turned

out to be the government itself. The capital's National Museum is packed full of artifacts spirited away from historic sites elsewhere, most of them in the Hejaz.

My rural trampings were motivated by a desire to see whether the people in the countryside were in any way different than their urbanized peers. I found that Saudis there felt the Kingdom's storied oil wealth had failed to trickle down to them. Villagers in the southern provinces of Asir, Jizan, and Najran complained bitterly that they continued to do without electricity as the royal family's profligate princes wasted spiraling sums on ever-more magnificent manses. Farmers in the north near the Jordanian frontier, while appreciating the subsidies enabling them to grow and sell fruits and grains to an expanding domestic market, chafed at being consigned to the lowest levels of a government-run monopoly, giving them no control over their own destinies. The few herdsmen I encountered resented Riyadh's frequent expropriations of land, acts which constrained their ability to graze sheep, goats, or camels, and that inexorably were leading to the passing of the pastoral way of life. It seemed to me that most, if not all, of the Hejazi hinterlands seethed with a palpable, if unspoken, anger at the authorities.

While having less, ostensibly, to complain about, Hejazis in the urban centers were equally frustrated. The difference is that they were far less reticent about expressing their feelings. After having spent time in both the cities and the countryside, I came to the conclusion that the Al Saud had lost touch with the latter's residents. The rulers were (and are) masterful at manipulating the local media and seemed to me to be equally adept at monitoring discontent in populous places like Jeddah. When, for example, Jeddawi sentiment in favor of the second Palestinian *intifadah* (uprising) in 2000 appeared to reach a fever pitch, the authorities allowed the press to run with various conspiracy theory–derived articles placing the ultimate blame for Israeli actions on the United States. The idea, according to my contacts in the media, was that the venting of the collective spleen against the sole superpower would function as a safety valve, enabling emotions to escape harmlessly into the ether rather than to stoke any nascent antigovernment sentiments.

The practice of manufacturing scapegoats for complex issues and then directing public sentiment toward them (and away from the rulers) is as old as empires. I contend, however, that it reached its full flowering only in the twentieth century, with the Al Saud at the top of the list of past masters. Unfortunately for the royal family, its aging leaders failed to recognize that the advent of the information age—ushered in by such innovations as the facsimile machine, CNN, and the Internet—changed the rules of the game forever. The Islamic Awakening of the early 1990s showed how the shrewd use of facsimile messages against the backdrop of CNN broadcasts of U.S. troops "occupying" the Muslim holy land could embolden an opposition movement. Less than a decade later, the Awakening's spiritual heirs—led by Usama Bin Ladin's al-Qa'ida— proved the Internet's power to unite and incite those who felt they had been wrongfully denied fortune, power, and glory.

And yet, throughout my time in the Kingdom, the Al Saud continued reflexively turning on and off the state media spigot, blindly trusting that this blunt means of exerting its considerable influence—coupled with good, old-fashioned repression—would yet again prove sufficient to contain any threats. The royals were right, for the most part. Saudis in large urban areas recalled the lessons of the past and proved susceptible once again to the government's blandishments and brutality. But the global media's reach proved long and intimate. The trickle down economics that failed to enrich the Hejazi hinterlands during the oil boom years were followed, 30 years later, by cascading newspaper, television, and Internet messages marinating recipients in the idea that the United States is the enemy of Islam. Lacking the credibility to counter the flow, the princes could only contribute to it. Longstanding grievances came of age under the tutelage of image-makers and storytellers with scores to settle and agendas to advance. Little effort was required to push a few of the more impassioned to the brink. As is now well known, 15 of the 19 hijackers involved in the terrorist attacks of September 11, 2001, were Saudis, with most hailing from the Hejazi hinterlands.

The four reports in this chapter encompass much of the diversity I encountered in the far-flung reaches of the Hejaz. The first details a visit to Tabuk, a northern province where life revolves largely around farming. My visits there (I made several with then-Consul General Richard Baltimore) revealed that Tabuk's rich historic heritage and natural splendor give it the potential to develop tourism as a supplement to its agricultural base. In the second report, I wrote about Najran, a southern province looked upon with mixed feelings by many Saudis. The locus of a monotheistic martyrdom celebrated in the Qur'an, it for years held out as the sole Christian stronghold in Muslim Arabia. More recently, Najran was an autonomous Ismaili shaykhdom until the collapse of the Ottoman Empire, when it became one of the prizes in the struggle between King Abd al-Aziz and Yemen's Imam Yahya. Its inhabitants remain incompletely reconciled to Saudi rule.

The third report is an account of a tour Baltimore and I made of the southern al-Baha province. The splendor of the mountainous landscape with its venerable stone villages, so startling to a visitor arriving from the flat coastal plain, is lost on locals eager to embrace modernity. Finally, the fourth report describes what I learned of the key role tribes continue to play in the Asir, an ethnically Yemeni southern province that is the Kingdom's most densely populated.

How Green Is My Valley (March 2000)

Tabuk, a Saudi governorate devoted to agriculture (and, to a lesser extent, military) pursuits, represents the Hejaz's northern terminus. The lifestyle of its residents, however, could hardly be more different that that enjoyed by their southern cousins. In contrast to Jeddah, where street-sweepers and U.S. Consulate employees are among the few who commence toiling before 10:00 a.m., Tabuk's workers are early risers who hit the fields at daybreak. Of course, they go to bed early, too, making the province seem a Hoosier-state hamlet compared with the western region's other urban centers, where dining before 8:00 p.m. is considered gauche and no self-respecting Saudi retires before the wee hours of the morning.

Following a meeting with Tabuk's governor, Fahd bin Sultan bin Abd al-Aziz, we were invited to stay at the Tabuk Sahara hotel (which he owns) and to visit two of the area's largest farms and several archeological sites. Surrounded by razor wire-topped fences posted with Education Ministry warnings against trespassing, most of the latter sites are off limits to all but authorized visitors. The tour encompassed points south, west, and north of Tabuk City, including portions of Qurayyat Governorate, the Kingdom's newest governorate.[2] One of the governor's protocol officers, Khalid Al al-Shaykh (a nephew of the Grand Mufti), served as guide, and a rustic from the southern town of Bisha named Fayez served as our driver. Notably, both carried pistols (in shoulder holsters) throughout the tour while verbally discounting the possibility of banditry or other unpleasant encounters with local tribesmen.

The tour began with a drive-by of Tabuk's Hejaz Railway station. Recently restored, portions of it are used as a municipal car park. It follows the same plan as the station in Medina but is not nearly so grand. Built of the sand-colored limestone blocks from which most of the other stations are constructed, it lacks the slightly fussy Ottoman charm of its dilapidated counterpart in the City of the Prophet. The next stop was the Governor's new office palace. This massive edifice, far larger than any other building in Tabuk, is scheduled to open in two months' time. Work on the eye-catching, Dallas-in-the-desert exterior is complete, but the interior appeared at least several months away from being finished. According to Khalid, the building's size is accounted for by the fact that 300 people work directly for Fahd bin Sultan in Tabuk, along with another thousand or so employees who are scattered in towns throughout the governorate.

Lunch was followed by a visit to Astra Farms. With a yield of 18 million stems per year (10 million carnations, 4 million roses, 1.2 million chrysanthemums, and the remainder a mix of irises and lilies), Astra is by far the Kingdom's largest flower producer. According to Khalid al-Kawas, Astra's plants and flowers production manager, the farm exports 15 percent of its yield, mainly to the Gulf and Eastern Europe. Escorting me through a number of greenhouses (including one in which the Nancy Reagan variety of chrysanthemum is grown), he made a point of noting that Astra even sends cut flowers to the Netherlands. He then provided a quick walkthrough of several non-flower greenhouses where lettuce and cucumbers are produced for the domestic market.

On the way to visit the farm's quail sheds (where 10 million of the birds are hatched annually), al-Kawas pointed out several bee hives—Astra produces an average of 5 tons of honey each year—and vineyards, where 6,000 tons of red globus grapes per year are harvested for domestic consumption. He concluded the program with a peek at the ranch house belonging to Astra's owner, Sabieh al-Musri, a Palestinian-Saudi who, as an early supplier of foodstuffs to the Royal Saud Land Forces, believed the troops should not have to rely on produce from Jordan and Syria. From a humble beginning of 12 hectares in 1965, Astra now boasts some 3,000 hectares under cultivation and 1,500 employees, perhaps 15 of whom are Saudis, according to al-Kawas. Most of Astra's lands lie north of Tabuk in Qurayyat Governorate.

The Tabuk Agricultural Development Corporation (TADCO) was next on our itinerary. It produces cereals and cash crops, particularly wheat, barley, alfalfa, fruits, potatoes, onions, and nuts. With 35,000 hectares under cultivation, TADCO is one of Saudi Arabia's largest farms. According to a map of the area, all of its lands are in Qurayyat Governorate. TADCO was started in 1983 as a joint stock corporation with 28,000 Saudi shareholders. Fahd bin Sultan currently serves as chairman of its board of directors.

TADCO's general manager, Saad Muhammad al-Swatt, told us the enterprise began by growing wheat and barley, both of which were heavily subsidized by the Saudi government. Both are less subsidized now, but the government has maintained strong price support for alfalfa to encourage its production. Al-Swatt said that barley (the Kingdom imports up to one-third of the world's supply) and alfalfa are used as feed by the massive dairies located outside Riyadh. TADCO's first cash crops included peaches, apricots, and apples. Standing before a site plan of the farm in TADCO's luxurious administrative offices (which include a sprawling, gilt-trimmed conference room), al-Swatt pointed out numerous 800-meter-diameter pivot fields (which appear from the air as green circles) of alfalfa and barley. We then embarked on a driving tour through extensive orchards featuring drip irrigation, almond trees (Spain is a major importer of the nuts), and olive groves.

During a brief look inside TADCO's 20,000-ton cold storage facility (the largest in the Middle East) and an apple sorting, grading, and crating room, al-Swatt noted that water is not a problem. TADCO has 126 wells, with water depth ranging from 100 to 150 meters below ground level (although, owing to variations in surface topography, some bores are as deep as 800 meters). Moving on to commercial issues, he said that even with TADCO's enormous economies of scale, farming is an inherently uncertain undertaking that cannot occur without government assistance. He described the disturbances at the World Trade Organization's meeting in Seattle as a wake-up call to global financiers who would like to treat agriculture like any other business. Until someone figures out how to eliminate weather-related risks and the vagaries of the commodities market, farmers will continue to rely on price supports and subsidies, he asserted.

Day two featured a partially off-road tour of ruins. The first stop was Qurayyah, northwest of Tabuk City, site of what is alleged to be a Roman temple complex overlooking the old spice route. Its fine, 2-meter-high, 2,000-year-old stone work has held up well. Several hundred meters away were some Nabatean petroglyphs and several caves dug into the shale hillsides. According to an Education Ministry official who acted as our docent, the Nabateans used the clay they excavated from the caves to make pottery. They may also have had kilns nearby; a few shards of broken pottery decorated with the distinctive Nabatean snake design were found just outside the caves, whose interiors were littered with human bones. According to the Education Ministry official, it is not clear how old the remains are, although they probably are pre-Islamic. We drove on to Mugheir Shuaib, also known as Medain Shuaib, which is located due south of Tabuk City near al-Bad. Home of 30 diminutive, picturesque Nabatean tombs carved into

The picturesque tombs carved into sandstone cliffs at Mugheir Shuaib predate Medain Salih and Petra, the two best-known Nabatean sites. (Author)

sandstone cliffs, it predates both Medain Salih and Petra.[3] Our docent observed that Mugheir Shuaib frequently is referred to by locals as the "little Medain Salih."

From al-Bad we continued further west to the low-lying Ras al-Shaykh Humayd headlands, which jut out into the Red Sea across

A derelict military seaplane rests on the sands of the windswept Ras al-Shaykh Humayd headlands in the Gulf of Aqaba. (Author)

from the Sinai Peninsula. There, the mouthwatcringly green-blue Gulf of Aqaba laps tawny sands. Despite its startling beauty, few Saudis visit the place, said Khalid, because a strong breeze constantly blows, wreaking havoc with *thobes* and *abayas* alike. At the tip of the headlands rests a derelict, U.S.-origin military seaplane. Listing on its belly with its landing gear retracted and one wing tip brushing the sand, it has been scoured clean of its original paint by years of exposure to the elements. Where it once had Royal Saudi Air Force or, perhaps, U.S. Navy markings, its aluminum skin now sports a crazy quilt of spray painted tags, such as "Mahmoud loves Layla."

Before returning to the hotel, we stopped at Dhat al-Hajj. A combination Hejaz Railway station and caravansary located just across the Tabuk Governorate boundary in Qurayyat (off the road that leads north to Jordan), its main attraction is a restored hostel-cum-fortress once used by pilgrims from the north seeking overnight shelter and protection from marauding tribes. Unlike most of the other Hejaz Railway stations in Saudi Arabia, this one still has intact track with rails and sleepers. The ticket office windows are hung with the original wooden shutters, and the half-derelict brick water tower retains its iron tanks. According to our driver, Fayez, Dhat al-Hajj's springwater is renowned for its pleasant taste and healthful properties. A sip from the public pump revealed it to be unexceptional, although certainly an improvement over Jeddah's sometimes mucilaginous—and always unhealthful—tap water.

Day three of the journey found us bounding across the desert southwest from Tabuk to Rawwafah, the site of a ruined temple said (by those who claim to have seen the now-missing lintel that graced its entrance) to have been dedicated to Roman emperor and stoic philosopher Marcus Aurelius Antoninus in 166. It resembles a smaller, and more tumbledown, version of the temple complex at Qurayyah. Until two years ago, it had been in good shape. At that time, according to the local *shaykh* (who was a toothless but exceedingly good-humored old gentleman), he was forced at gunpoint by unknown tribesmen to open the gate in the fence surrounding the site so that they could unearth the gold they believed lay under the temple floor. None, of course, was found, and their careless excavation resulted in the collapse of fully half of the structure. The Education Ministry official confided quietly to me that he suspected the *shaykh* was in on the scheme, because it was unlikely anyone other than locals whom the old man recognized would have known about or been able to find the isolated temple. Upon hearing my comment about how the area—judging by its flat floor and the "bathtub ring" on the

The ruined Rawwafah temple, southwest of Tabuk, is said to have been dedicated to Marcus Aurelius in 166. (Author)

surrounding cliffs—appeared to have been a seabed once upon a time, the *shaykh* asserted that indeed the region was long ago submerged under a body of water referred to locally as the "Tito Sea."

After our docent bid farewell, a drive to a village called Dissah, reputed to contain a Nabatean-style tomb and other antiquities, followed. Dissah lies at the southeastern end of Wadi Qaraqir, between Rawwafah and the seaside village of Muwaylih. Getting there was easy: A new, paved road leads to Dissah by an indirect, but far smoother, route than the old dirt track off the coastal road. However, locating what a contact described as remarkable ruins proved more difficult. After passing through Dissah twice (where many of the houses were festooned with the green-and-white al-Atawa tribal flag), the tour finally spied an Education Ministry–style fence straddling a small, rocky bluff behind the village. Upon investigation, the site (which, without our docent, we were forced to enter by wriggling beneath the bottom of the fence and some soft sand) had only an unremarkable, recently patched-up rock hut with a wooden door and the half-finished facade of a small and rather unimpressive Nabatean tomb. Our attempts to find other sites of historical interest in and around the village were in vain.

Nonetheless, our venture northwest from Dissah into the heart of Wadi Qaraqir itself proved anything but fruitless. The valley opened into a canyon with sheer, red sandstone walls. Dotted with towering, eroded rock pillars; watered by springs trickling from the cliffs into a small stream; and carpeted with palm groves, thick rushes, oleander, and wild lemon trees, it is a heart-achingly lovely place. We stopped for a picnic beneath a stand of cypresses and watched the sun cast violet shadows across the cinnamon rocks while swallows flitted and soared, their cheerful cries occasionally drowned out by the surprising number of vehicles struggling to make their way along the rough, wet canyon floor. An attempt to follow the path taken by the other vehicles to what we presumed would be the old dirt track back to the coastal road was unsuccessful; our car was low on gas, daylight was fading rapidly, and the terrain became steadily more impassible. Back down Wadi Qaraqir and through Dissah once more, the group retraced its path and arrived at the hotel in Tabuk in time to for the Consul General and I to pack and catch the last flight to Jeddah.

Land of Water, Fire, and Ire (April 2000)

The fiercely independent nature of Najran's population belies the idyllic aspect of this ancient land, which features three fertile *wadis* (the

Najran, the Badr al-Janub, and the Habona) in which water flows several months of the year. Located 1,000 kilometers south of Riyadh, the governorate is bordered by mountains to the north (the Salim Ridge), west (featuring Al-Mahdiq, or the crevice, in which waters from the peaks of Yemen descend), and south (the Najran Ridge, site of 1,450-meter Mount Abu Hamadayn). To the east lies the Rub al-Khali, or Empty Quarter, the planet's largest ocean of sand.

Najran in Arabic has at least two meanings. It is a term used to describe the wooden frame on which a door opens and is also a synonym for thirsty. Local tradition has it that the land derived its name from the first man to settle in the area, Najran bin Zaydan bin Saba bin Yahjub bin Yarub bin Qahtan. The governorate is famous among Muslims because of a story of monotheistic martyrdom related in the Qur'an. In *surah* 85 ("The Constellations"), the following verse appears:

> By the heaven with its constellations!
> By the promised day, by the witness
> And that which is witnessed!
> Cursed be the diggers of the trench,
> Who lighted the consuming fire
> And sat around to watch the faithful
> Being put to the torture!

The incident described occurred in 525. Dhu Nawas, head of the Himyar state in Yemen, conquered Najran, which had been an important stop on the spice route from Hadhramaut (eastern Yemen). At that time, Najran was a Christian kingdom governed by a bishop named Aretas. Himyar was Jewish, and Nawas demanded that the Najranis convert to his faith or die. Many refused to adopt Judaism, and Nawas ordered his armies to surround them. A trench was dug, filled with oil, and set ablaze. The Najranis again were given the opportunity to convert. Once more refusing, they were pitched into the inferno. The present-day village of al-Ukhdud, outside Najran City, is the reputed site of this drama.

Among Saudis, admiration for the stubborn faith of the Najranis is tempered by the recollection that most refused to embrace Islam during the lifetime of the Prophet. Some Najranis escaped from Nawas' armies and martyrdom in the trench. One of these, Daou bin Thaban, sought assistance from the Byzantine Emperor who, along with Ethiopia's leader, saw this as a propitious opportunity to increase their influence on the Arabian Peninsula. An army of 7,000 men, led by Abraha al-Ashram, the Christian viceroy of the Negus of Abyssinia, crushed Nawas' forces and restored Christian rule in Najran, which prospered as the most important Christian enclave in Arabia.[4] Prefiguring Paul Revere's ride by nearly 1,200 years, its inhabitants—not wishing to experience another conquest—took to hanging lanterns in its numerous church steeples to warn of approaching enemies.

In the early seventh century, Muhammad sent emissaries to Najran seeking its inhabitants' acceptance of Islam. There were few takers. A generation later, Caliph Omar Ibn al-Khattab decreed that Islam was to be the sole religion of the Arabian Peninsula and forced Najranis who would not embrace the faith to leave; many resettled in the Levant. Some Ismailis subsequently fled to Najran and Yemen after the failure of the Qarmatians (an Ismaili sect that at one point seized Mecca, removed the Kaaba's black stone, and ruled over what is now the Eastern Province and Bahrain) to maintain their hold on power in the wake of Salah al-Din (Saladin) ibn Ayyub's conquest of Egypt in 1171, which put an end to the Ismaili dynasty there. South Arabia's mountains were an ideal sanctuary because of their distance from Islam's bloody internecine struggles. Maritime advances had long since rendered the spice route obsolete, thereby enhancing the region's isolation.

Also troubling to Saudi Muslims, and to Hejazis in particular, is the fact that Najran once attempted to usurp Mecca's position as a place of pilgrimage. According to legend, on the summit of Mount Taslal, 35 kilometers east of Najran City, lay the ruins of the Najran Kaaba. Built by Banu Abd al-Madan bin al-Dayan al-Harithi along the same design as the Kaaba in Mecca, it served for 40 years during the pre-Islamic era as an alternative pilgrimage site for traders traveling the spice route. The Najran Kaaba was destroyed in the year 24 by a Roman army dispatched on the orders of Augustus Caesar.[5] In the wake of his occupation of Egypt, the Emperor sought absolute control over the spice trade and viewed Najran and its pilgrimage as a threat to commercial stability. To ensure that his resolve was not underestimated, Caesar ordered Najran City pillaged and burned.

Perhaps what most bothers the Kingdom's Wahhabi majority is that the Ismailis, as Shia, practice deliberate dissimulation called *taqiyya*.[6] This doctrine permits them to pretend to be Sunnis—to the extent of adopting typically Sunni names—to protect themselves and their families from harm. To some Wahhabis, *taqiyya* makes it impossible to trust Shia and renders them a virtual fifth column undermining the integrity of the Saudi state.

Under the Ottoman Turks, Najran existed as an autonomous Ismaili shaykhdom. With the collapse of the Empire after World War I, Najran became one of the prizes in a struggle between two expansionist leaders: Yemen's Imam Yahya and King Abd al-Aziz. In the early 1930s, the Al Saud won control of the area, along with the Asir and Jizan, by sending an army (led by Ibn Saud's second-oldest son, the future King Faysal) to meet and defeat the forces of Sanaa's doddering Hamid al-Din dynasty. Like the other conquered southern provinces, Najran culturally is more Yemeni than Saudi; tribal and religious ties link its population to the south and not to the north. In 1982, Interior Minister Nayif bin Abd al-Aziz dedicated Saudi Arabia's then-largest dam, Al-Madhiq, on the *wadi* of the same name just upstream from the ruins of a dam built during the time of the Queen of Sheba (tenth century B.C.E.). Al-Madhiq is 260 meters long, 60 meters high, and can retain more than 86 million cubic meters of water. Conceived of in Riyadh as a way to regulate water flow into the *wadi*, thus ensuring the steady irrigation of crops, it is regarded by some Najranis as a symbol of Saudi hegemony.

Najranis are celebrated (albeit quietly) in the Kingdom for their singing, dancing, and storytelling. The vigorous Dance of the Horses, used to brace warriors for battle, makes the Najdi sword dance look flaccid by comparison. The Rafza Dance, accompanied by an insistent drum beat and shrill pipes, sometimes features more than 1,000 men. It is used to commemorate feasts and marriages. Najrani storytellers center many of their tales around a mythic character named Bouzid al-Hilali, who is said to have resided in al-Ukhdud. Stories about him frequently are humorous and teach moral lessons, and in this way are similar to the folk tales popular in Egypt.

See Rock City (November 2000)

On a crisp morning, we drove southwest from Jeddah for more than five hours to Bisha, a town in the northeastern Asir not far from the Wadi al-Dawasir. Bisha, site of the Kingdom's largest dam and renowned for the quality of its dates, proved an ideal starting point for a journey into al-Baha. Like prosperous communities throughout the Hejaz, Bisha has been developed so completely that few physical traces remain of its traditional past. Al-Baha, by contrast, has not yet succumbed to the pressures of modernization, perhaps because it has had little perceived value to offer Saudis, much less foreigners. However, with the government now tapping tourism as a new revenue stream, al-Baha may prove to be in the catbird seat. Its diverse landscape could prove a magnet to tourists seeking a taste of a relatively unspoiled Arabia.

The old Governor's Palace in Najran, now a museum, showcases the unique architectural style of the region. (Author)

One climbs slowly, almost imperceptibly, west from the warm, lush Wadi Bisha toward a forbidding-looking spine of the horizon indicating the Sarawat range. A first-rate (albeit two-lane) highway clogged with lumbering Mercedes-Benz diesel lorries takes the traveler into al-Baha

Governorate past streams, terraced fields, and stone watchtowers. The latter were used by farmers of old to protect their crops; rapacious neighbors, not marauding Bedouin tribesmen, inspired the construction of literally thousands of such rocky redoubts. On approaching the al-Baha City municipal limits, the altitude increases quickly and baboons appear along the roadside. Much of the eastern portion of the governorate lies on a 1,000-meter high plain, but the capital and its environs are perched amid the Sarawat's tallest peaks, with an average elevation of 2,000 meters.

As befits their city's name (which means lake bed or river bottom in local parlance), al-Baha's half million or so residents live in fairly new houses and apartment blocks lining both sides of a shallow, green valley. A modest business district snakes along the valley floor. The governor's palace is set atop one of several granite fingers rising from the lowlands; the al-Baha Palace Hotel and a futuristic motel dominate the summits of two others. The city has a sleepy aspect even during the morning rush hour. Farming and herding remain the area's main occupations, but light industry (including the Kingdom's largest sponge factory) is a growing component in the local economy. Tourism has not yet turned al-Baha's plows into Palm Pilots, but it has the potential to contribute to the governorate's bottom line, particularly during the summer months when Saudis unable or unwilling to travel abroad look for a respite from the brutal heat of the Hejaz.

Al-Baha City's unassuming air may stem from the fact that it is an accidental capital. According to local lore, the governorate's two major tribal confederations, the Ghamid and the Zahran, argued bitterly over which would have the honor of playing host to the governorate's new seat after it was annexed by the Al Saud in the early 1930s. In one of the Solomon-like gestures for which King Abd al-Aziz was known (hagiographically, at least), he split the difference and declared that al-Baha, halfway between the Ghamid and Zahran lands, would be the capital of—and lend its name to—the new governorate.

After our arrival in town, we toured two of al-Baha's main attractions. The first was Baljurashi, some 30 kilometers southeast of the capital, a site famed for its venerable camel steps. These hewn granite risers cling precipitously to the flank of the Sarawat and lead down into a broad expanse of the Wadi al-Baha. Until relatively recent times it was the only direct route for caravans up the escarpment and into the highlands, and its existence was known to but a few outsiders (including the explorer Johann Lewis Burckhardt, who climbed the trail in circa 1814). Today, it is used mainly by goatherds. After driving west through the narrow, hilly village of Baljurashi proper, we arrived at a parking lot held aloft by two Sarawat pinnacles. By retracing our route on foot eastward for 100 meters, we were able to slip behind a 2-meter-high concrete wall that conceals a garbage dump from the road. After wending our way through the trash (which had everything including, literally, a kitchen sink) for about 30 meters, we arrived at the top of the camel trail and were bowled over by a breathtaking vista.

The full expanse of the Wadi al-Baha is laid before one as the camel steps wind steeply down the slope of the Sarawat. It is as if the world suddenly falls away at the visitor's feet, revealing what was once a robust riverine environment. A broad, flat bed lolls languidly on the valley floor, where it is joined by the tentacles of tens of tributaries funneling down between multiple modest mountains. The contrast between the dark, scrub-forested sides of the valley and the gray-white wash left by the long-gone waters is stunning. Descending the steps several hundred meters, we were refreshed by a cool, anis-scented breeze.

The steps are in excellent repair and it is possible to follow them all the way down to the bottom. During our visit, the place was silent save for the scrambling hooves of several goats as they foraged among the rocks. Aside from the steps, the only other signs of human habitation were occasional pieces of windblown trash and one or two tiny towns on the southern rim several kilometers away across the valley. With some cleanup and care, Baljurashi could easily become a national park that tourists—domestic hotel-hoppers and foreign trekkers alike—would pay good money to experience. Unfortunately, local inhabitants appear to regard it as little better than a convenient dumping ground.

From Baljurashi we drove northwest to Dhee Ayn, site of a "floating village." The attraction is a venerable stone settlement set atop a white marble stump in the middle of a palm-fringed pocket canyon. It is located near the terminus of the main escarpment road that takes one from the al-Bisha highlands to the governorate's western frontier at the scalding al-Tihama coastal flats. In a contrast nearly as striking as that which meets the visitor's eyes in Baljurashi, the dark, somber-looking dwellings of Dhee Ayn appear to defy gravity by levitating atop a crystalline cloud. The settlement is abandoned and unguarded, and one may drive right up and climb its ramparts and explore the chilly rooms within its numerous, multistoried houses and towers. However, because the village is built out of heavy shale slabs supported by desiccated timbers, it is less than stable. The floors within some of the structures have caved in; many others tilt at precarious angles. The sturdy-looking outer walls are deceiving, and visitors would do well to restrain the urge to do too much poking about.

Although its walls and ramparts are approachable and appear to be in good condition, Dhee Ayn is unstable, with heavy shale slabs supported by desiccated timbers. (Author)

As at Baljurashi, signs of human visitation were scarce at Dhee Ayn. But a small parking lot nearby sporting four permanent plastic picnic canopies suggested that the site is a more popular draw during the summer tourist season. The lack of explanatory and cautionary signage was disappointing, as was the fact that no one would be able to stop an unscrupulous visitor from collecting a few souvenir stones. The results of such looting were clearly visible in several less-than-spectacular stone settlements along the road leading back to Jeddah. Tumbled-down towers and walls next to modern concrete structures incorporating old slate slabs as decoration bore witness to the indifference with which local inhabitants regard their architectural heritage.

Tribalism in the Asir (February 2001)

Tribal identities are strong in the Asir, a mountainous and intermittently green governorate in southwestern Saudi Arabia whose topography, flora, and fauna are reminiscent of the area around California's Joshua Tree National Park. Asiris, however, are anything but laid-back, approaching life with an almost manic gusto. Indeed, the region long has been known for the fiercely independent nature of family confederations that for millennia resisted advances by outsiders while quarreling incessantly with one another.

I spoke with a number of locals in the Asir about the region's tribes. All agreed that the most powerful is the Qahtan. Organized like a Scottish clan, the Qahtan is composed of numerous families (including the al-Shareef, the Fehayd, the Mushayt, and the al-Odadi) who traditionally lived in the highlands. The head of the clan is always the eldest male member of the al-Shareef family. Currently, Ahmad bin Husayn al-Shareef, the governor of al-Namas (a hamlet some 150 kilometers north of the Asiri capital of Abha and overlooking the Wadi Khat), is the Qahtani *shaykh*.

The Qahtani's chief rivals are the men of the Shahran, another highland tribe. According to a Qahtani who has researched tribalism in the Asir, the Shahran was the region's ruling clan under the leadership of the Ibn 'Ad family until about 120 years ago. The Ibn 'Ad insisted on governing not only the mountain folk but also the inhabitants of the coastal lowlands or Tihama. These people, some of whom to this day live in African-style straw huts and make their livelihood growing herbs and vegetables, are referred to as "flower people" by the highlanders. In part this name mocks the lowlanders' lack of tribal affiliations, but it also reflects the tribesmen's genuine admiration for the vibrant culture (not to mention freer lifestyle) of the Tihama.

In the 1880s, the Ottoman Turks attempted to assert greater control over the Asir. The province was at the time an independent principality presided over by the self-styled "King of the Asir," Muhammad Ibn 'Ad. In an attempt to break his will, the Ottomans captured some of

Qahtanis, like this guide, are intimately familiar with and zealously protective of their tribal lands in the Asir highlands. (Author)

King Muhammad's relatives, including his beautiful and intelligent daughter, Zaynab. She was imprisoned in Istanbul, where she wrote from memory a complete edition of the Qur'an before collapsing with fever and dying. According to the Qahtani with whom I spoke, the book still exists in the Turkish archives.

Back in the Asir, Zaynab's capture had the desired effect, and King Muhammad agreed to negotiate with the Ottomans beneath a grove of cypress trees outside his capital at Siqa (in the al-Sawdah heights about 10 kilometers northwest of Abha). The wily ruler dressed himself and two retainers in identical clothes and rode out to meet the Turks, who could only guess which was the real king. Legend has it that as the parties sat in the tall grass and parleyed, a snake slithered up the ruler's robes, ultimately reaching his chest. Unable to ignore it any longer, King Muhammad reached down his shirt, pulled out the serpent, and strangled it to death before his bug-eyed interlocutors, who knew at once that he was their man. They arrested him on the spot and took him off to Istanbul in chains. As the party wound its way down the escarpment to ships waiting at the coast, the flower people, who had been mercilessly taxed by the king, showered him with satiric verse. The erstwhile monarch, beaten but unbowed, reportedly cursed the lowlanders and predicted that they would be fated to live under a succession of tyrants worse than he.

Ottoman rule in the Asir lasted until near the end of World War I. The Qahtan tribe moved into the power vacuum that followed the Turkish withdrawal and successfully repelled three attempts by King Abd al-Aziz to conquer the region. At the same time, Yemen's Imam Yahya sent emissaries (and, later, forces) aimed at persuading the Asiris that their best bet was to cast their lot with him. Wishing only to be left alone, the Qahtanis found themselves in a pickle: As the Al Saud pressed from the north and the Yemenis from the south, the Shahran were preparing to fight to see that the heirs of King Muhammad (who, like his daughter, perished in a Turkish prison) would again assume leadership of the Asir. The stalemate was broken when then-Prince Faysal bin Abd al-Aziz won over the al-Shareef *shaykh* by promising the Qahtanis perpetual preeminence (and jobs) in exchange for fealty to the Al Saud. Cleverly, Faysal pointed out the lack of viable alternatives to Saudi rule, implying that Najdi overlordship was the lesser of three evils. The Qahtanis capitulated and the Al Saud annexed the Asir without firing another shot.

Tribes today still play an important role in the Asir. Most inhabitants identify themselves with one or another clan, with many local government functionaries and businessmen claiming Qahtani affiliation. Even a few inhabitants of the Tihama boast tribal affiliations. Some say they are affiliated with the Bani Shihr (a tribe that historically resided in both the highlands and the valleys), the region's third-most-powerful confederation after the Qahtan and the Shahran.

According to several Qahtanis with whom I spoke, the tribes continue to perform the traditional functions of organizing community projects, mediating disputes, and dispensing charity. One al-Odadi, for example, explained to me that tribal *shaykhs* are responsible for ensuring that terraces are maintained on the mountainsides, that stone walls dividing fields are kept in good repair, and that workers (usually foreigners) are hired to dig drainage ditches. The *shaykhs* receive a small monthly stipend from Asir Governor Khalid al-Faysal for these services. When disagreements erupt among families within a tribe, it is the *shaykh*'s job to mediate.

A member of al-Namas Amir Ahmad bin Husayn al-Shareef's staff told me that his boss spends upward of one-third of his time keeping peace within the Qahtan tribe. He added that the problem of feuds is handled by the collection of "taxes." Families are assessed monthly at the rate of 100 riyals ($26.67) per male household member over the age of 12. This has proven more than sufficient to cover blood-money expenses that average 125,000 riyals per incident. Intertribal disputes, by contrast, are settled by Asir's governor; the February 14 edition of the English-language daily *Saudi Gazette* featured an article describing how a feud in Khamis Mushayt was settled on Khalid al-Faysal's orders. According to the *amir*'s staffer, a program launched five years ago by the governor, wherein financial incentives are offered to encourage intermarriage among the tribes, has not proven successful.

Tribal tax proceeds not used to settle blood feuds are directed by the *shaykh* to charitable endeavors, such as supplementing dowries, assisting poorer families caring for widows and orphans, and purchasing expensive medicines and equipment for the elderly and the disabled. The *amir*'s staffer said the tribe even had managed to make a modest donation to the government's fund to assist the "Palestinian freedom fighters."

CHAPTER 6

Rhyme and Reason

Translation is like a séance with the dead and
what comes out on the planchette will often read
like urgent nonsense.

—Robert Irwin

To almost all Muslims, most especially to Saudis, the Qur'an is the
immutable, unalterable, and unbowdlerized word of God. It was
received in its present state, directly from the heavens, through the
Archangel Jibril (Gabriel) to the Prophet Muhammad. It is held as the
final testament, the clearest explication of human rights and responsi-
bilities. No man-made document can supersede it; man-made laws
cannot trump God's divine diktat. To question the Qur'an's authority
or authenticity is blasphemy, and translating the Qur'an is deemed
impossible. Arabic is the language of God, and human attempts to
render what He said into another tongue inevitably will produce
errors. Islam, the most recent of the great monotheistic religions, was
born in Arabia, but Arabic is the mother tongue of fewer than 10 percent of its adherents today, meaning that most adherents effectively are
shut out of a complete understanding of their faith.

   The Qur'an is an extended prose poem. Muhammad was born at a
time when few could read or write (he himself was illiterate). History
and tradition were conveyed in verse, with pre-Islamic bards earning a
living and winning renown by traveling the trade routes to compose
heroic odes for tribal chieftains and sappy stanzas for lovelorn lotharios.

The poet was the prince of artisans and the power he exercised over the people frequently was deemed subversive. Some of these bards were executed by suspicious rulers, and the Qur'an itself warns Muslims against being seduced by silver-tongued devils with nefarious agendas.

It is ironic, then, that the Qur'an itself is regarded as the supreme achievement of Arabian poetry. Following a complex-yet-hypnotic metric style, and employing repetition and rhyme to hammer home its tenets, the Muslim holy book—particularly when recited by a skilled *khatib* or Muslim cantor—transports the listener to a meditative state. Details move to the background, and it seems that God is speaking through tones and colors. The medium becomes the message: harmony, among people and between humans and their maker, is paramount.

In light of the Qur'an's poetic potency, the inability of most Muslims to comprehend the book would be of little consequence if its particulars were as clear as its advocates insist they are. But they manifestly are not. Scholars following widely divergent interpretive traditions have flourished for centuries by puzzling through the Qur'an's thicket of contradictions and cryptic allusions. Not written down until nearly a century following the Prophet's death, the book's verses are beautiful but often confoundingly inconsistent. Some seem intended, like a Buddhist *koan*, to do no more than stir reflection. Indeed, the earliest and shortest *surahs* (found, inexplicably, at the back of the book) are haiku-length treatments of grand themes. These frequently are the focus of believers, like the Sufis, who seek to understand God through the Qur'an's esoteric essence.

The longer chapters at the front of the book, meanwhile, have less to do with provoking deep thoughts than instructing humans how to organize and administer an Islamic society. These *surahs*, of course, are championed by those—principally the Wahhabis—for whom the exoteric word of God is everything. For these literalists, a Muslim need do little more than read and obey.

So it is that Wahhabis clerics, as bedeviled as anyone by the Qur'an's lack of clarity, have come to rely heavily on the *sunna* and the *hadith*—Muhammad's practices and his words and deeds as recounted by his companions—to figure out what to do in any given circumstance. Although advocates for a pure, unencumbered, and austere faith, they quickly devolved into caricatures of woolly headed, how-many-angels-can-dance-on-the-edge-of-a-pin theologians. Moreover, because their idol lived more than 1,400 years ago, the conclusions they draw invariably reflect a medieval outlook. *Bida'* or innovation in the faith, like translation of God's word from Arabic, is to be avoided at all costs. The Wahhabis I knew were stained to the core with an implacable conservatism, usually coupled with an abiding hostility toward those whose more modern outlook challenged the foundations of the faith as they interpreted it.

Wahhabis in the Kingdom and elsewhere are in denial concerning the fact that the Islam they extol is as much an interpretation as any other. The Qur'an does not speak for itself and it is further handicapped by the lack of authority accorded translations. In a Muslim world without a caliph or other supreme authority, various "experts" have taken it upon themselves to tell the faithful what to believe. Because they speak Arabic, because they come from the land of the two holy cities, and especially because they enjoy access to virtually unlimited funds, the backward-looking Wahhabis rule the roost. Their take on the Qur'an is the most widespread today, and they continue to fuel zealots and extremists the world over. It is the ultimate conundrum that these verse-hating Luddites have extended their dominion by exploiting stanzas from a holy book that warns, repeatedly, against the power of poetry.

It seemed appropriate to me to end with a selection of contemporary Saudi verse. Nothing I found served as well as the following doggerel penned by Asir Governor Khalid al-Faysal, which manages to capture perfectly the at-once worldly and parochial people I knew as Hejazis. His Royal Highness—a friend of Britain's Prince Charles and generally seen as among the most broad-minded of the Al Saud—dashed off this work and had it printed in the Hejazi daily *Al-Madina* in response to U.S. criticisms of the Kingdom's human rights record. I translated and reported it to Washington in an unclassified dispatch that same month.

Human Rights (April 2000)

To every concerned Muslim
To every dignified Arab
To every Saudi proud to be a Muslim:

If they accept it or do not accept it,
We only have the rights of our Islam.

If they speak, get mad or threaten,
We will never abandon our religion.

We will never bargain with our principles.
Even if we die, our book is our constitution.

Even if they do not declare it,
We know their goal is to spread vice among us.

Why do we accept everything they export?
Why do we have to lose our values?

Why do we have to accept their lies
And abandon for their sake our traditions?

I wish they did not promote their rights.
I wish some of our people did not sell out.

Unfortunately, they voted for corruption.
You people be witness and tell the world:

Our law is Islam and God is our god.
We have not but the law of our God.

Notes

INTRODUCTION

1. The Islamic Awakening movement was led by religious figures who had had enough of "business as usual" in Saudi Arabia. Epitomized by radical clerics Salman al-'Awda and Safir al-Hawali, its members regarded the Al Saud as impious and King Fahd's use of Western forces to defend the Kingdom following Iraq's invasion of Kuwait in 1990 as proof that the royal family was unfit to rule in the name of Islam. Antigovernment protests erupted in several cities in response to venomous sermons by Awakening leaders distributed throughout Saudi Arabia on cassette tapes. A brutal crackdown on dissent, launched in 1994, effectively put an end to the movement by the following year.

CHAPTER 1

1. A friend and colleague at the U.S. Consulate in Jeddah, David Kelly, died in a car crash in July 2002, days after I had returned to Washington. His remains were returned to the United States.

2. The Saudi wedding ceremony is brief, encompassing only the conclusion of a binding contract to which both bride and groom may add conditions, frequently including the circumstances under which a divorce may be sought (the divorce rate in the Kingdom approaches 60 percent). For example, many brides stipulate that they are free to divorce should their husband take another wife. Once the contract is signed by the groom and the bride's

father or other adult male representative in the presence of a judge or imam recognized by the court as qualified to render binding religious opinions, the ceremony is complete. The bride returns to the female guests to primp and party with them until the agreed time she is to rendezvous with her new husband, usually at the groom's father's home, to consummate the marriage.

3. The Saudi government does not keep official statistics concerning the numbers of unmarried men in the Kingdom. However, anecdotal information supported by tribal tradition suggests that, by the age of 30, almost all Saudi men—including homosexuals—have married at least once, if only to maintain appearances.

4. C. Niebuhr, *Reize Naar Arabie en Andere om Ligxgende Landen* (Amsterdam: S.J. Baalde, and Utrecht: J. Van Schoonhoven and Co., 1776).

5. Information on Huber's life is contained in David G. Hogarth's *The Penetration of Arabia: A Record of Western Knowledge Concerning the Arabian Peninsula* (New York: F.A. Stokes, 1904) as well as in the preface to Huber's own *Journal d'un Voyage en Arabie 1883–84* (published under the auspices of the French Ministry of Public Instruction, 1891).

6. Some Hejazis of the era were Christians or Jews, but many followed versions of the Yemeni Sabean faith and worshipped the moon god.

7. The Mamelukes' defeat prompted an Egyptian Diaspora in the Red Sea. Several thousand émigrés settled in Yanbu—the port for Medina—where their influence on local art and architecture is noticeable to this day.

CHAPTER 2

1. Each summer, from the mid-1990s until 2002, Saudi Arabian Airlines added nonstop, jumbo jet flights from Riyadh to Orlando. The Nordstrom department store at the Tysons II shopping center in suburban Washington, DC, continues to play host to busloads of BMOs—black moving objects, as head-to-toe swathed Saudi matrons sometimes are dubbed—each year when school lets out.

2. Arabs, like Sephardic Jews, are Semites, but the term has acquired more a religious than an ethnic connotation.

3. Volcanic activity last occurred near Medina in 1256. In that year, a huge lava flow came within 4 kilometers of the city.

4. The lack of reliable data concerning births of Saudi princes, let alone princesses, and the Al Saud's general reluctance to discuss the matter, have left analysts with little choice but to guess at the family's actual size. Estimates range from 3,000 to 60,000 members. Official U.S. observers believe 30,000 (roughly half male, half female) is a reasonable figure, based on what is known about the family's composition and birth rates within the Kingdom.

5. Medina, like Jeddah, once boasted of many historic homes. Unlike those in Jeddah, however, nearly all were torn down within the last decade in the name of progress. Owners were bought out and their lands consolidated to make room for commercial projects financed by princes and wealthy merchants.

6. Some scholars suggest he may have done so at the behest of Abdallah ibn Ubayy, leader of the so-called hypocrite faction of Muslims that bridled at Muhammad's political leadership.

7. The Bani Shayba continue in this role. Interestingly, their name means "the sons of Sheba," and some Hejazis speculate that the tribe found its way to Mecca during the eponymous queen's legendary expedition to meet King Solomon.

8. Some Hejazis claim that a crucifix, portraits of Jesus and the Virgin Mary, and a menorah also once graced the Kaaba's interior.

9. A similar system of *qanats* once brought water to Jeddah from Wadi Fatima to the city's southeast.

10. Burton's adventures in the Hejaz are recounted in his *Personal Narrative of a Pilgrimage to Al-Madinah and Meccah [1893]* (New York: Dover, 1964).

CHAPTER 3

1. Muslim women undertaking the pilgrimage are not required to wear special clothes, only plain versions of their ordinary costumes and no jewelry, makeup, or fragrance.

2. Hajj Minister Iyad Madani in 2001 quoted me an average mortality rate of 9.6 percent for the preceding five pilgrimages.

3. The other pillars are *shahadah* (profession of faith), praying five times daily, fasting during Ramadan, and giving alms.

4. This is in addition to the *hadi* pilgrims are required to provide in commemorating *Eid al-Adha* or the Feast of the Sacrifice.

5. The latter portion of the *takbir* frequently is mistranslated as "God is great" or "God is the greatest." Neither is correct; the Arabic usage is a clear example of a relative and not an absolute comparative. The semantic difference means that no matter what claims people of another faith may make for their deities, God is always "greater," that is, he forever is in a position to trump any other god.

CHAPTER 4

1. A Jeddah-based newspaper that is the Kingdom's most-popular paper.

2. A less-popular Hejazi daily perpetually on the brink of insolvency.

3. The royal family reckons that the present Saudi Kingdom, which began with Ibn Saud's reconquest of Riyadh in 1901, is the third to have existed since the mid-eighteenth century.

4. The Saudis, as Wahhabis, view themselves as "nonimitators" or "not attached to tradition" and therefore not answerable to any school whatsoever, observing instead what they regard as the practice of early Islam. However, by this very attitude they achieve the ideal of Ahmad ibn Hanbal, for whom the Hanbali school was named, and thus are regarded as part of the Hanbali tradition. In the Wahhabi conception, Islam should be based solely on the twin pillars of the Qur'an and the *hadith*. Consistent with the views of the eighteenth-century founder of their puritanical sect, Muhammad ibn Abd al-Wahhab, Wahhabis reject scholarly interpretations as "innovations" that corrupt the faith.

5. A prosperous Jewish settlement near Medina, Khaybar was sacked and its residents were massacred by an army led by Muhammad in 628. According to British Muslim convert and Qur'anic translator Muhammad M. Pickthall, "After the Muslims' victory at Khaybar, a Jewess prepared a meal of poisoned meat for the Prophet. He tasted, but did not swallow, a small piece of it and then told his comrades that it was poisoned. One Muslim, who had already swallowed some of it, died instantly. The Prophet, even though he had only tasted it, contracted the illness that eventually caused his death. When the guilty woman was brought before him, she said she had done it to avenge the humiliation of her people. The Prophet forgave her." *The Meaning of the Glorious Qur'an,* revised and edited by Arafat K. El-Ashi, PhD (Beltsville, MD: Amana Publications, 1996), xxvii.

6. *Jinn* are better known to Westerners as genies.

7. Iblis is identifiable with Lucifer, the fallen angel and God's enemy.

8. R.W. Emerson, *Poetry and Imagination* (1872).

9. F. Van der Linden, *The Real Reagan* (New York: Morrow, 1981), p.31.

10. Shortly after this report was disseminated, its last paragraph was leaked (presumably by an official in Washington) and published in the *Washington Times*.

11. Saudis do not use the terms "Wahhabi" or "Wahhabism," viewing them as pejorative. If pressed to draw a distinction between themselves and other Muslims, they say they are *muwahidoun*—literally unitarians—a reference to their insistence on God's indivisible nature. Some prefer the word *salafiyin*, which implies a conscious imitation of the "pious ancestors" of early Islam. This term is used most often to describe hardcore Wahhabis, such as the Taliban and the Saudi religious police known as the *mutawwa'in*.

12. The calendar then in use had 360 days. The annual hajj festival made up the difference in the solar year. All conflict was forbidden within a 16-kilometer radius of the Kaaba during the hajj.

13. According to one of my contacts (a Hejazi historian), the goddess al-Lat had three aspects. These were al-Lat herself, "the Maiden," symbolized by a waxing crescent moon and representing fertility; al-Uzza, "the Mighty"

full moon representing protection; and Manat, "Destiny," the waning moon of wisdom and prophecy. The moon goddess was represented by the black stone still embedded in a corner of the Kaaba. She was attended by seven priestesses who circumambulated the Kaaba (naked) seven times, once for each of the known planets. Each of her aspects had an individual temple as well. The Maiden was worshipped in bacchanal style amid the vineyards and rose gardens kept by wealthy Meccans in Ta'if; the Mighty had a shrine to the southeast in the town of Nakhal where sacrifices of animals were common; and Destiny was venerated at Qudhaydh, a no-longer extant village on the Red Sea coast between Mecca and Medina, where devotees performed divination by casting seven arrows and reading the resulting patterns. Another temple dedicated to the phallus god *Dhu al-Khalasah* ("he who has substance," represented by a carved piece of white quartzite) is said to have existed at a place called al-Waliyyah (near the present-day northern Asir town of Tabalah), a seven nights' journey from Mecca on the way to Sanaa. Its focus was Canopus, the brightest star in the Hejazi heavens after Sirius. Reportedly the site of ritual prostitution, Dhu al-Khalasah's temple was maintained by the Banu Umamah clan of the Daws tribe. Interestingly, the Kaaba is aligned to permit accurate sightings of both the new moon and Canopus. The crescent and the star continue to feature prominently in Islamic symbology.

14. The excesses of Wahhabism's proponents during the first Saudi occupation of Mecca and Medina in 1803 produced widespread antipathy toward the creed.

15. Hejazi forbearance was not without limits. On June 30, 1858, Jeddah's Muslim population rioted in reaction to British policy in the Red Sea area. More than two dozen Christians, including the British and French consuls and members of their families, were killed.

16. Jeddah's low-profile Sufis so far have managed to avoid such difficulties.

CHAPTER 5

1. The Najd is the central, and most isolated, region of Saudi Arabia. Next to its largest city, Riyadh, lays the ruined mud-brick village of Dir'iyyah, the ancestral home of the Al Saud. Like other capitals founded for political purposes (Brasilia, Ankara, and Islamabad, to name a few), Riyadh has sought to bolster its legitimacy by legislating a commercial *raison d'etre*. For example, in 2002 the rubber-stamp *Majlis al-Shura* (Consultative Council) endorsed a royal edict declaring that all customs activities related to shipping would be transferred from the Jeddah Islamic Port to landlocked Riyadh, an expensive and nonsensical maneuver (albeit a boon to the trucking sector) meant to compel more companies to move their headquarters to the capital.

2. Qurayyat Governorate has yet to be identified on most maps, including those—like the one in this volume—produced by the U.S. government.

3. Medain Salih, a magnificent Nabatean tomb city about 200 kilometers north of Medina, is surpassed only by Petra, the famed "rose-red city, half as old as Time" in southern Jordan that was featured in the movie *Indiana Jones and the Last Crusade*.

4. Abraha went on to earn infamy among Muslims for a failed attempt to destroy the Kaaba. Having built a magnificent cathedral in Sanaa, Abraha intended his expedition to eliminate its primary pilgrimage rival in Mecca. Hejazi legend holds that three ornate, cedar ceiling-support posts inside the Kaaba, intended for Abraha's cathedral, were scavenged when the ship transporting them sank in a storm off the coast of present-day Asir. According to the Qur'an's *surah* 105 ("The Elephant"), God defeated Abraha's army—which featured an elephant used to terrorize the locals—by causing birds to pelt the invaders with "stones of baked clay" (possibly pottery shards). The year of this event, 570, known as "the year of the elephant," traditionally is held as that of Muhammad's birth.

5. During a visit to Najran in February 2002, I climbed Mount Taslal, which appeared to be remnants of a long-extinct volcano. I found nothing atop its several eroded peaks that would suggest it had ever held a site of ritual veneration. However, at the floor of the cone and accessible only via several ground-level entrances barred by barbed-wire fences, there is a flat, open space the size of several soccer pitches. A structure the size of the Kaaba in Mecca would fit neatly into it, with ample room to spare for circumambulation. Several Ismaili contacts later told me that Taslal, in fact, is not where their Kaaba was located. Although refusing to divulge its whereabouts, they claim it still exists and that it was a focus of worship among the Ismailis as recently as the 1960s.

6. The Ismailis sometimes are called "sevener" Shia because they take as their spiritual redeemer Ismail, the seventh imam after Muhammad.

Glossary

As the container of Arabian culture, Arabic interposes itself in any attempt to understand the Saudis. Because Arabic contains sounds and structures not used in English, and because it generally is written without vowels, transliterating it into English is an exercise in inexactitude and frustration. Scholars, newspapers, governments, and agencies within governments—including our own—adhere to different conventions, so it is possible to see Jeddah rendered as "Djedda," Medina as "Madinah" and Mecca as "Makkah." I strived in my reporting to include definitions wherever possible; however, I include the following glossary of some of the most significant and frequently occurring words, with the less-familiar terms in italics.

abaya: The neck-to-ground black cloak worn by Arabian women in public.

abd: "Slave of" or "servant of." It is not a pejorative term and is part of many male names referring to various attributes (the so-called "99 names") of God. Abd al-Aziz, for instance, means "slave of the Powerful."

afreet: An evil *jinn* (genie) that has become powerful.

al: The article representing "the," which is attached to the following word with a hyphen. Thus, *al-kitab* is "the book." The l is elided when joined to certain consonants, however, so it is possible to see *al-sayara* ("the car") written as *as-sayara*.

Al: The article for "house of" or "family of," used to identify princely tribes such as the Al Saud. Always capitalized, it is not hyphenated and the l is never elided.

Al-Fatihah: The Qur'an's opening chapter; it encapsulates the Islamic creed and is recited every time a Muslims prays.

al-Jazirah: Literally "the island," the Arabic name for the Arabian Peninsula.

amaar: A *jinn* (genie) that lives among humans.

amir: Also seen as *emir*, an honorific denoting a commander, ruler, or tribal chief.

arkaan: The four indispensable rites of the hajj imcumbent upon all pilgrims.

Ashura: The tenth day of the Muslim calendar, observed by Sunnis with fasting because such was the practice of the Prophet. For Shia, *Ashura* marks the martyrdom of Muhammad's grandson Huseyn at Karbala, Iraq. Their ritual grief is expressed through bloody spectacles of self-flagellation.

'asr: Afternoon prayers.

bida': "Innnovation" in the faith, a term Wahhabis apply to practices and activities they find objectionable.

bin: Literally, "son of," sometimes rendered as Ibn. It can be part of a tribal name, such as Bin Ladin, and also is used between given names and patronymics. Hence, Fahd bin Sultan bin Abd al-Aziz Al Saud means "Fahd, son of Sultan the son of Abd al-Aziz of the House of Saud." A Saudi official told me in 2000 that a "pureblood" Arab male should be able to recite his lineage back at least nine generations. The plural of bin is bani.

bint: The feminine form of bin, used to denote "daughter of." It also means "girl." Its plural is *banat*.

bir: The word for a water well. The plural is *abyar*.

birqat: A masonry pool or water basin along the hajj route from Iraq.

caliph: The Prophet Muhammad's rightful successor, as regarded by Sunni Muslims. The caliphate is the institution of the caliph, much as the papacy is the institution of the pope.

da'wa: Literally "invitation," it is Islamic proselytizing. Wahhabi Muslims in particular believe it is their duty to call not only non-Muslims, but other, "hereticai" Muslims to the "pure Islam" they see themselves as practicing.

Day of Judgment: The culmination of the "end of days" when all humans will be bodily reconstituted and summoned from their graves to account for their lives before God.

dhuhr: Midday prayers.

eid: The word for "feast." *Eid* al-Fitr is the "feast of fast-breaking" that celebrates the end of the fasting month of Ramadan, and *Eid* al-Adha, "feast of the sacrifice," is the culmination of the hajj (pilgrimage to Mecca).

fajr: Dawn prayers.

fatwa: An edict regarded as a binding injunction under Islamic law. Only people regarded as having sufficient scholarly credentials may issue *fatwas*.

ghutra: The Bedouin male headdress, consisting of a large square of cloth folded in half diagonally and held in place with a black cord looped around the head known as an *iqal*.

ghul: The term for a hideous *jinn* (genie) from which the English word ghoul derives.

hadi: Literally "gift," this term refers to the animal a pilgrim sacrifices (or, more frequently, pays to have slaughtered) during the hajj.

hadith: A verified narrative originating with one of the Prophet's contemporaries that describes the words or of example set by Muhammad. Although the plural is *ahadith*, I use *hadith* for both singular and plural.

hajj: The annual pilgrimage to Mecca that takes place during the eighth through thirteenth days of the twelfth month (Dhu al-Hijjah) of the Islamic calendar. It is one of the five pillars of Islam (the other four being *shahadah* or the profession of faith, praying five times daily, fasting during Ramadan, and alms-giving) and is required of all Muslims to perform once in their lifetimes if they are physically and financially capable of doing so.

haram: A term meaning "forbidden" or "prohibited," it is used to demarcate the Muslims-only zones around Mecca and Medina.

Haramayn: the term used to refer to the two holy cities of Mecca and Medina.

Hejaz: Western Saudi Arabia. Historically, it denoted a strip of land, 200 kilometers at its widest point, stretching from north of the border with Jordan down to just south of Mecca. Today, it generally is considered to be those lands bounded by the Red Sea and the escarpment marking the interior plateau that extend from the Jordanian border south to the Asir Governorate. Residents of the Hejaz are called Hejazis.

hijra: The date at the end of September, 622, when Muhammad fled Mecca for Medina, marking the start of the Islamic calendar.

hisn: The word for "fort."

Iblis: Lucifer, the fallen angel and God's enemy.

ifraad: One of three hajj varieties in which the *umra* rites are omitted

ihram: The physical manifestation of a pilgrim's intent to perform hajj or *umra*. For men, it consists of two seamless lengths of white cloth, one worn around the waist and the other draped over one or both shoulders. For women, it is a plain version of their ordinary costume.

ijtihad: Interpretation of Islamic doctrine.

imam: In the parlance of Sunni Muslims, this term means "prayer leader." In theory, any adult Muslim male can fulfill this role. In practice, the eldest or most-esteemed person in any nonmosque setting will be expected to lead prayers. Most mosques have at least one salaried, "official" imam. For Shia Muslims, the term imam refers to one regarded as a leader of believers or *the* leader, that is, the Prophet's rightful successor, and corresponds to the Sunni concept of the caliph.

intifadah: Arabic for "uprising," the term denoting violent Palestinian resistance to Israeli rule.

isha': Evening prayers.

Ismailism: A branch of Shia Islam which posits that the seventh imam (after the Prophet) was the *mahdi* who will return to restore righteousness on earth just before the Day of Judgment. Adherents are called Ismailis.

jabal: The word for "mountain."

jahaliyya: The "age of ignorance," as Muslims regard the pre-Islamic era.

jamaraat: Three pillars near Mecca representing Satan and his temptations at which pilgrims ritually cast pebbles during the hajj.

jamrah: The singular form of *jamaraat*.

janna: The Arabic verb meaning to hide or to conceal.

jihad: Struggle in the way of Islam. Generally used to connote the effort one exerts to be a better Muslim and the spread the faith, it figures prominently in the duty of believers to defend Islam from its enemies by all means necessary and thus can be interpreted as "holy war." Some Muslims, particularly extremists, reckon jihad as the "sixth pillar" of Islam.

jinn: In the Islamic cosmology, beings made of smokeless fire. Although seldom seen, *jinn* inhabit the earth with humans and can lead people astray or cause them harm. They are known in the West as "genies."

Kaaba: The cube-shaped, black-draped, stone-block building at the center of the Grand Mosque in Mecca toward which Muslims direct their prayers. Islam holds that it is the original house of monotheistic worship established by Adam after he and Eve were ejected from the Garden of Eden. It is believed to have been rebuilt by Noah, then Ibrahim (Abraham) and his son, Ismail (Ishmael), and finally reconsecrated by Muhammad.

kabsa: The Saudi national dish, consisting of mutton and rice.

khatib: A Muslim cantor or prayer reciter.

kiswa: The embroidered black shroud that covers the Kaaba.

koan: a paradoxical statement or question used by Zen Buddhists in meditations to aid in escaping dependence upon reason and acquiring intuitive insight.

maghrib: Sunset prayers.

mahdi: The messiah figure in Islam who will restore righteousness on earth just before the Day of Judgment.

maher: Dowry or bride-price.

mahram: A related male escort who accompanies a single female during the hajj.

majlis: The word for "council." *Majlis al-Shura* means "consultative council" and is the appointed assembly that substitutes for a legislature in Saudi Arabia.

Manichaeism: A school of religious thought, prevelant in the Middle East before Islam, positing that good and evil necessitate one another and than humankind can only understand and escape this dualistic struggle through asceticism.

mawlid: The Prophet's birthday, a major feast day in the Hejaz before the imposition of Wahhabism.

mimbar: The pulpit from which an imam addresses congregants in a mosque.

miqaat: One of five ritual ablution points in the Hejaz, marking the boundary where pilgrims must assume *ihram* before approaching Mecca. The plural is *mawaqeet*.

miswak: A fibrous twig harvested from the desert-dwelling *siwak* tree that Arabs have used for millennia as a combination toothbrush and dentifrice.

Monophysitism: An early Chrisitian philosophy holding that Jesus was altogether divine even though he had temporarily acquired an earthly form.

mufrid: A person performing the *ifraad* hajj.

muhrim: A person in the state of *ihram* or ritual purity.

mutawwa: A member of the Saudi religious police charged with enforcing public morality. The plural form is *mutawwa'in*.

muwahidoun: Arabic for "unitarians," the term Wahhibis most commonly use to distinguish themselves from other Muslims.

Nabatean: The term used to denote an ancient Arabian civilization, which at its zenith stretched from Damascus to Yemen. In the first century, it became a Roman client state and subsequently was made a province of the empire and dubbed *Arabia Petraea*.

Najd: The central region of Saudi Arabia. Encompassing the Kingdom's conservative heartland, it was the birthplace of Wahhabism and is home to the Al Saud ruling family and the capital, Riyadh. Residents of Najd are called Najdis.

qal'at: Literally "castle," a term Hejazis applied to the caravansaries along the hajj trail from Damascus.

qanat: An underground water channel.

qareen: The invisible *jinn* (genie) counterpart of each human.

qarin: A person performing the qiraan hajj.

qasida: An Arabian ode.

qibla: The direction of prayer. In Islam, believers must face the Kaaba (Mecca) when worshipping God.

qiraan: One of three hajj varieties in which the umra and hajj rites are performed together.

Qur'an: Often rendered elsewhere as Koran, the Muslim holy book. It is regarded as the literal word of God as dictated to Muhammad in Arabic. Translating the Qur'an is deemed impossible because the process would introduce human error.

rak'aat: Prostrations, the touching of the forehead to the ground during Muslim prayers.

sahih: Authentications, the term for something that is a settled fact.

Salafism: The belief that the time of the *salafiyin* ("pious ancestors"), that is, the era of the Prophet and his first four "rightly guided" successors, was the apotheosis of Islam. Salafism has much in common with Wahhabism and it frequently is difficult to distinguish between the two. An adherent is a *salafi*.

sayy: The hajj ritual emcompassing the seven one-way trips a pilgrim completes between the hillocks of al-Safa and al-Marwa in the Grand Mosque.

sayyid: An honorific given to one who is able to trace his bloodline back to Muhammad through the Prophet's grandson Huseyn.

shahadah: The Muslim profession of faith. To convert ("embrace Islam"), one must recite the following before at least two believers, preferably at a mosque: "I bear witness that there is no god but God and Muhammad is the messenger of God."

Sharia: Islamic law. Its corpus is composed of the Qur'an and the *hadith*, with occasional reference to the *sunna*.

sharif: An honorific given to one who is able to trace his bloodline back to Muhammad through the Prophet's grandson Hassan. The Hashemite ruling family of Jordan (and formerly the ruling family of Iraq and of the Hejaz) claims such descent.

shaykh: Sometimes rendered elsewhere as sheikh, a leader or chieftain. The term frequently is used to denote people deserving special reverence, such as religious authorities.

shaytan: Literally "satan," a devil.

shayateen: The plural form of *shaytan*.

Shiism: The "heterodox," minority trend within Islam, making up roughly 10 percent of believers who insist authority passed by blood from Muhammad via his son-in-law Ali to his grandson Huseyn and so on.

Adherents (singular and plural) are called Shia; the word itself means "partisan."

shirk: Polytheism or associating others with God, the worst sin a Muslim can commit.

sidir: A type of desert thorn bush.

siwak: A desert-dwelling tree from which *miswak* sticks are harvested.

souk: An Arabian marketplace.

Sufism: The mystical branch of Sunni Islam, the adherents of which believe the Qur'an is replete with hidden meanings and that certain devotional practices (such as chanting, spinning á la the "whirling dervishes," and the like) produce trance-like states enabling one to commune directly with God. Practitioners are called Sufis.

sunna: Literally meaning "tradition," this term refers to the day-to-day practices of the Prophet, such as sleeping on the right side and trimming one's mustache but not one's beard.

Sunnism: The "traditional," majority trend within Islam, including perhaps 90 percent of the faithful who believe authority in religious matters passed from the Prophet Muhammad to his companions and then others through the process of *shura* or consultation. Adherents are called Sunnis.

surah: A chapter in the Qur'an.

takbir: A formulaic expression used especially during hajj, translated as "in the name of God, God is greater".

talbiyyah: A verse recited by hajj pilgrims that goes, "Here I am. O God, here am I. There is no partner with You. Here am I. Surely, all praise and graces are with You, and so is the dominion! There is no partner with you."

tamattu: One of three hajj varieties in which the *umra* rites are performed before the hajj rituals.

taqiyya: A Shia doctrine permitting believers to pretend to be Sunnis to protect themselves and their families from harm.

tarawih: A lengthy recitation of Qur'anic verses that occurs every evening during Ramadan.

tawwaf: Circumambulation of the Kaaba.

thobe: The white, neck-to-ground shirtdress worn by Arabian males.

tihama: The flat, featureless coastal plain south of Jeddah.

ulama: Saudi Arabia's official clerical establishment.

umma: The community of believers, used in reference to Muslims writ large.

umra: The so-called minor or "off-season" pilgrimage, it consists of the Grand Mosque rituals. Its performance earns blessings but does not satisfy a Muslim's requirement to perform the hajj.

velayat-i faqih: The Shia concept of "the mandate of the jurist" which entails a top-down interpretation of doctrine.

wadi: A dry river valley subject to flash-flooding when it rains.

Wahhabism: The puritanical sect of Sunni Islam to which most Saudis subscribe. It is named for Muhammad ibn Abd al-Wahhab, an eighteenth-century itinerant preacher who inveighed against the "innovations" corrupting the "pure Islam" he envisioned was practiced in the time of the Prophet and his early successors. His cause was boosted by support from Muhammad Al Saud, a local tribal chieftain who saw in Abd al-Wahhab's radicalism a vehicle for extending his dominion in the Najd. Their partnership and the intermarrying of their progeny produced the dual dynasties—the Al al-Shaykh ("House of the Shaykh") having primacy in religious matters, and the Al Saud ("House of Saud") holding sway in governance—that dominate the Kingdom to this day.

wajibaat: Duties.

wudhu': Standard pre-prayer ablutions, involving the washing of the face, hands, and feet.

Zoroastrianism: An ancient Persian faith, still extant, which posits that a supreme god, Ahura Mazda, requires the good deeds of humankind to defeat his nemesis, the evil spirit Ahriman.

Bibliographic Note

I prepared for my sojourn in the Hejaz by researching Islam and Arabia before and after the establishment of the Saudi Kingdom. In the main, this involved reading reams of classified and unclassified reports produced by various U.S. government agencies, including the Department of State. My readings also included numerous books and journals, in whole or in part. Foreign Service reporting guidelines, however, discourage annotation in general and reference to other published works in particular: "We're paying you to tell it like it is, not to tell us what someone else thinks," is a standard Foggy Bottom refrain. Had I known from the outset of my tour that I would produce this volume, I would have kept a detailed record of publications I consulted; a few are mentioned in the text or notes of some of my dispatches (I relished bending the reporting rules whenever possible). As for those not specifically mentioned, I seek the reader's indulgence and plead for understanding. Foreign Service Officers—generalists charged with ingesting vast amounts of information, making heads or tails of it, and quickly conveying a seamless and internally consistent message in a policy-relevant form to Washington before moving on to the next item in a never-ending stream of reporting requirements—are singularly disadvantaged when it comes to retrospectively explaining how, beyond what they have been told, they came to know what they know.

Nonetheless, the indispensability of several works made them unforgettable and obliges me to give them special mention. First, of course, is the Qur'an itself. I used a composite of my own translations and those of Muhammad M. Pickthall from *The Meaning of the Glorious Qur'an*, revised and edited by Arafat K. El-Ashi, PhD (Beltsville, MD: Amana Publications,

1996). For the *hadith*, I relied on translations provided by Hejazis, principally two contacts (one an avowed Wahhabi, the other a Sufi, both affiliated with Jeddah-based Islamic nongovernmental organizations) whose knowledge of English surpassed my facility in Arabic. The *Concise Encyclopaedia of Islam* (London: Stacey International, 1989) by Cyril Glasse offers the best layman's introduction to the beauty and complexity of Islam. No one, I think, has explained the Arab mind better than David Pryce Jones in *The Closed Circle: An Interpretation of the Arabs* (Chicago: Ivan R. Dee, 2002). For those interested in Arabic poetry in translation, Robert Irwin's *Night and Horses and the Desert* (New York: Anchor, 2002) is a superb compilation spanning pre-Islamic odes to modern verse. My understanding of contemporary Saudis was enhanced by Peter Theroux's wry, eye-opening *Sandstorms: Days and Nights in Arabia* (New York: W.W. Norton & Co., 1991). Theroux also has performed a signal service for those of us whose Arabic is too weak to allow for pleasure reading in that tongue. His masterful translation of Abdelrahman Munif's *Cities of Salt* trilogy (*Cities of Salt*, 1989; *The Trench*, 1993; *Variations on Night and Day*, 1994, all published by Vintage in New York) makes accessible this all-too-rare work of Arab historical fiction, one that—like others challenging the Riyadh-approved version of the Kingdom's history—is banned in Saudi Arabia.

Index

Page numbers in italics refer to photos.

Abd al-Aziz bin Fahd, Prince, 86–89
Abd al-Hamid II, Sultan, 32
Abd al-Majeed, Prince, 83
ibn Abd al-Wahhab, Muhammad, 99
Abdallah, Crown Prince, 70
ablution points. See *mawaqeet*
Abraha al-Ashram, 114, 134n4
Abrams, Elliott, 84, 85, 87, 88
Abu Rashed, Khalid, 80
agriculture, 105, 106, 108–9, 118;
    government assistance, 109
Ahmad bin Husayn al-Shareef,
    121, 124
Al al-Shaykh, Salih bin Abd al-Aziz,
    84, 85, 86
Al Saud, 13, 88–89, 99–100, 130n4,
    131n3, 133n1; control by, ix, x,
    xiv–xv, 14–15, 88–89, 100, 105–6,
    133n1; and education, 13, 14, 15,
    100, 104; and hajj, 14, 48–50, 99;
    and the media, ix, 49, 105–6; and
    renovation/expansion, 26, 29, 32,
42 *(see also* modernization); rule of
    the Hejaz, 13–14, 105–6; rule of the
    Hejaz, in al-Baha, 118; rule of the
    Hejaz, in Asir, 116, 123; rule of
    the Hejaz, in Najran, 106,
    114–16; unification, xiv, 99–100;
    and U.S., xv–xvi, 87, 127–28; and
    Wahhabism, xiv, xvi, xvii, 14,
    100–101, 132n4, 132n11 *(see also*
    Wahhabis)
alcohol, banning of, 9, 14
Ali ibn Husayn ibn Ali al-Hashemi,
    99
Allah. *See* God
Americans: and hajj, 59–60, 69;
    view of Saudis, xv. *See also*
    non-Muslims
al-Anbariyya Mosque, 26–27
angels, 77, 79, 97
Arab Revolt, 13
Arafat, 52, 56, 67; Jabal al-Rahmah,
    63. See also Day of Standing
archeological artifacts, 104–5;
    Tayma Stone, 8–9

archeological/historical sites, 104; in
al-Baha, 118–21, *120*; Darb
Zubaydah (*birqats*), 37–41;
destruction by Wahhabis, 15, 100;
King Solomon's Mines, 37; King's
Highway (*qal'ats*), 31–37; in
Mecca, 94 (*see also* Grand
Mosque); in Medina, 24–27, *27,
28*; in Najran, 116, *117*; Okaz
market, 40, *41*; in Tabuk, 107,
109–13, *110, 111, 112*
architectural examples: *birqats*,
38–41, *39*; homes, 18; markets,
40, *40*; *mawaqeet*, 41–46, *42–46*;
mosques, 26–27, *26*; palaces, *117*;
qal'ats, 33–36, *34, 35, 36*; railway
stations, 26–27, *27*, 107; settlement walls, *120*; temples, 112, *112*;
tombs, 109–10, *110*
Asir, 107, 121–24, *122*
Astra Farms, 108

Al-Baha, 107, 116–21, *120*
Baljurashi, 118
Baltimore, Richard, 106
Bani Hashim (tribe), 96
Bani Qurayza (tribe), 25
Bani Shayba (tribe), 29, 131n7
Bani Shihr (tribe), 123
Banu Umamah (tribe), 98,
132–33n13
Battle of Ohud, 24
Battle of the Trench, 24–25
Bin Ladin, Usama, 95, 106
birqats, 37, 41; Birqat al-Aqiq, 38;
Birqat al-Khurabah, 38–39, *39*, 43;
Birqat al-Madiq, 38, 40–41. See
also *mawaqeet; qal'ats*
Bisha, 116
Black Stone, 20–21, 55, 98, 115. *See
also* Kaaba

bride-price. *See* dowries
Burton, Sir Richard, 38

caravansaries. See *qal'ats*
Catholics, 85, 87, 88. *See also* non-
Muslims
cemeteries. *See* Non-Muslim
Cemetery
children: births, 3; custody of, 81
Christians, 11, 96–97; explusion of,
90–91; rule in Najran, 106,
114–15. *See also* Catholics; non-
Muslims
clothing, xiv; *ihram* garments, 30,
52; and Wahhabis, 14, 100
consulates, history of, 12–13

Daou bin Thaban, 114
Darb Zubaydah, 37–41, 66
Day of Comfort, 56
Day of Judgment, xvi, 50, 86, 92
Day of Sacrifice, 56, 58
Day of Standing, 30, 52, 56, 66–67,
68
Dhat al-Hajj, 111
Dhee Ayn, 119–21, *120*
Dhu Nawas, 114
Dir'iyyah, 133n1
Dissah, 113
divorce, 81–83, 129–30n2. *See also*
marriage
dowries, 3–7; financial assistance,
4–7

economy, xvii, 14–15, 18; agriculture,
105, 106, 108–9, 118; economic
divide, xiv–xv, 3, 105, 106; hajj
revenue, 14, 99 (*see also* pilgrimage
trade); oil revenues, xv, 14–15;
shipping, 133n1; tourism trade,
17, 19

education, 13, 73; control of, 14, 15, 100, 104
eid, 14, 54; Eid al-Adha, 54, 56, 69, 131n4
eid rites, 57
Elgindy, Khaled, 84
evil eye, 77–78. *See also* magic

Fahd, King, 26
Fahd bin Sultan bin Abd al-Aziz, 107, 108
faith healers, 76. *See also* magic
Faysal, King, 116
Faysal, Prince, 123
financial aid. *See* government assistance
fortunetellers. *See* magic

God, 11, 73–75, 92, 97
government assistance: agriculture, 105, 108–9; dowries, 4–7; *kiswa*, 29; tribes in the Asir, 124
Grand Mosque, 20; during hajj, 54–55, 69; takeover, 100. *See also* Kaaba

hadi, 52, 57, 131n4
hadiths, 51, 89–91, 126, 132n4; compilations, 89–91; concerning expulsion of non-Muslims, 85, 89–91; concerning hajj, 51–52; concerning jinn, 93; and Quba'a Mosque, 26; schools of thought, 68, 89, 100, 132n4
haircuts, 52, 53, 54, 57, 69
hajj, 20, 47–71; administration of, 12–14, 48–50, 59–61, 71; crime during, 62; crowds, 20, 71; deaths, 50, 71, 131n2; history of, 10–14, 31, 51, 97, 99; by locals, 43, 46, 48, 54; preconditions for, 51–52, 58;

revenue, 14, 99 (*see also* pilgrimage trade); routes, 21, 53 (*see also* Darb Zubaydah; King's Highway); types of, 54, 56, 57. *See also* hajj rites
Hajj Ministry, 49, 59–60, 61
hajj rites, 52; Day of Standing, 30, 52, 56, 66–67, 68; *hadi*, 52, 57, 131n4; haircuts, 52, 53, 54, 57, 69; *ihram*, 30, 41, 43, 45–46, 52–54, 57; lapidation, 52, 57, 58, 68–69, 70–71; *sayy*, 52, 55–56, 57, 65; *tawwaf*, 52, 54, 55, 57, 58, 64–65, 69, 132–33n13
Hamza ibn Abd al-Muttalib, 24
ibn Hanbal, Ahmad, 132n4
al-Haramayn Foundation, 4–5, 7
Harun al-Rashid, 37
al-Hejailan, Salah, 80
Hejaz, xiii, 10, 13, 37, 104, 114
Hejaz Railway, 32–33; station in Medina, 26–27, 27, 28, 32–33, station in Tabuk, 107, 111
Hejazis, xv, 11, 12; in al-Baha, 116; and the Al Saud, xvii, 15, 105–6, 116, 133n14 (*see also* Al Saud); and Americans, xv, xvii; in Asir, 121–23; cultural identity, x, xvi–xvii, 2, 10–15, 18, 37, 73–74, 79, 99, 121, 127–28; future of, x, xviii, 15, 18, 100–101; in Najran, 113–15, 116; religious tolerance, 10–11, 96–97, 99, 100; in Tabuk, 107; and Wahhabis, 100, 133n14; and Westerners, xvii, 18; youth, 15
Huber, Charles, 8–9, 130n5
Hugronje, C. Snouck, 9
Husayn ibn Ali al-Hashemi, 13

Ibn 'Ad, 121–23
Ibn Saud (King Abd al-Aziz), xiv, 13, 29, 99, 116, 118, 123

Ibrahim, 96
idols, 10, 11, 31, 96–97; destruction
    of, 96–97; Hubal, 97–98. *See also*
    hajj: history of
ihram, 30, 41, 43, 45–46, 52–54, 57.
    See also *mawaqeet*
Imru al-Qays, 40
Interior Ministry, 49, 77
International House of Law (IHL),
    80
Islam: future of, 100–101; history of,
    11, 19, 24–26, 31, 96–100, 115;
    interpretation of doctrine, 84; and
    other religions, 89–91 (*see also* reli-
    gious freedom); pillars (of faith),
    51, 131n3, 132n4. See also
    hadiths; Muhammad; Qur'an;
    sunna
Islamic Affairs Ministry, 3–5, 7
Islamic Awakening, xv, 100, 129n1
Islamic law. See *Sharia*
Ismail, 55, 96
Ismailis, 106, 115, 134nn5–6;
    discrimination against, 100

Jabal al-Rahmah, 51
Jeddah Lawyers Association, 80
Jews, 11, 19, 96–97; expulsion of,
    90–91; in Medina, 19, 25, 96, 98,
    132n5; in Najran, 114; in the
    Qur'an, 19. *See also* non-Muslims
jinn, 77, 79, 91–95; at Birqat al-
    Madiq, 38, 39
al-Jinn Mosque, 94
Juhayman al-Utaybi, 100

Kaaba, 20–21, 131n8, 132–33n13,
    134n4, 5; attempted destruction
    of, 32, 134n4; Black Stone, 20–21,
    55, 98, 115; cleansing of, 98; dur-
    ing hajj, 54–55; history of, 11, 20,

97, 132–33n13; key, 29, 30; *kiswa*,
    27–31, 40; in Najran, 11, 115;
    security of, 22
Ka'b bin al-Ashraf, 25
Khalid al-Faysal, 124, 127–28
Khaybar, 132n5
al-Khayf Mosque, 61
King's Highway, 31–37
kiswa, 27–31, 40. *See also* Kaaba

lapidation, 52, 57, 58, 68–69, 70–71
al-Lat, 97–98, 132–33n13
legal system, 79–83; control of, 100;
    divorce, 81–83; judges, 81, 100;
    lawyers, 79–80; modernization,
    83; and religion, 74, 84–86 (*see
    also* religious freedom). See also
    Sharia

magic, 74, 75–79, 93. See also *jinn*
al-Malik al-Adil, 32
Malik ibn Anas, 89–90
Maqam Ibrahim, 65
al-Marayati, Dr. Laila, 84, 86
marriage, 1, 3–7, 129–30n2, 130n3;
    intertribal, 124; wedding con-
    tracts, 82, 129–30n2. *See also*
    divorce
mawaqeet, 21, 38–39, 41–46, 53;
    Abyar Ali, 41–42, *42*, 53; al-
    Juhfah, 42–43, *43*, 53; al-Sayy al-
    Kabir, 44, *45*, 53; Dhat 'Irq, 43,
    53; Hisn Juhfah, 33–34, *35*, 42;
    Wadi Murim, 43, *44*, 53;
    Yalamlam, 44–45, *45*, 53. *See also*
    birqats
McCarrick, Cardinal Theodore, 84,
    85, 87
McFarland, Steven, 84
Mecca, 19, 21; during hajj, 51, 52,
    54; history of, 10–12, 13, 24–25,

31, 96, 97–98, 99, 131n7; modern-
    ization, 61. *See also* Grand
    Mosque; hajj
Medain Salih, 110, 134n3
Medina, 18–19, 21–27; during hajj,
    51, 58–59; history of, 11, 18–19,
    24–26, 32, 96, 98, 99, 130n7,
    130n3 (chap. 2), 131n5. *See also*
    Prophet's Mosque
Mina, during hajj, 51, 52, 56, 57,
    58, 61, *62*, 70
miqaat. See *mawaqeet*
Mishari bin Abd al-Aziz Al Saud,
    Prince, 9
modernization: and Al Saud, 100,
    105–6, 131n5; communications,
    61, 106; computers, 61, 83, 106;
    legal system, 83; railway, 32; reno-
    vation/expansion, of cemeteries,
    8; renovation/expansion, of *kiswa*
    factory, 29; renovation/expan-
    sion, of *mawaqeet*, 41, 42; renova-
    tion/expansion, of mosques, 26,
    29, 61; renovation/expansion, of
    railway stations, 33, 107
moon goddesses. *See* al-Lat
Mount Taslal, 134n5
Mugheir Shuaib, 109–10, *110*
Muhammad, 96, 100; in battle, 19,
    24–25, 132n5; and hajj, 11, 31,
    51, 68; and *jinn*, 94; and Kaaba,
    21, 98; and *kiswa*, 28; and Mecca,
    11, 19, 24–25, 31, 96–98; and
    Medina, 11, 19, 24–26, 96, 98;
    and moon goddesses, 97–98; and
    Najran, 115; and other religions,
    89–91, 96–98; and *qibla*, 26; and
    Quraysh, 11, 24–25, 96–98; and
    women, 1, 25, 96–97
Mujallid, Khalid bin Muhammad,
    59

mutawwa'in, 14, 85–86, 132n11. *See
    also* Wahhabis: control by
Muzdalifah, during hajj, 51, 52, 56,
    57, 61

Najran, 97, 106, 113–16, *117*; and
    the Al Saud, 106; as alternative
    pilgrimage site, 115
Nakhal, 98
Namira Mosque, 61
Nassibah, 24
Nayif bin Abd al-Aziz, 49
Niebuhr, Carsten, 7
Night of Power and Destiny, 20, 22
Non-Muslim Cemetery (NMC), 2,
    7–9
non-Muslims, 130n6; expulsion of,
    89–91; right to worship, 84–89,
    95. *See also* Catholics; Christians;
    Jews

oil revenues, xv, 14–15, 106
Okaz, 40; market ruin, *40*
Omar ibn al-Khattab, Caliph, 90, 91,
    115
Ottoman Empire, 12–13, 29, 99,
    106, 115, 121–23; and Hejaz
    Railway, 32; and *qal'ats*, 32
Ousman, Cyril, 9

Perfumed Column, 23
pilgrimage. *See* hajj; *umra*
pilgrimage trade, 2, 10–14, 19,
    96–97, 99, 115; hajj vendors, 23,
    42, 69, 70, 71
pilgrims: Americans, 59–60, 69;
    encampments, 61–62, *62*; treat-
    ment of, 12, 49–50. *See also* hajj;
    pilgrimage trade; tourism
poetry, 25, 125–26; on the *kiswa*, 40
polytheism, 59, 76, 93, 96, 98, 100

Prophet's Mosque, 22–24, 59;
    Sacred Chamber, 22, 31
protests/uprisings: anti-U.S. protests,
    50; Arab Revolt, 13; Iranian
    Revolution, 100; Islamic
    Awakening, xv, 100, 106, 129n1;
    Palestinian intifadah, 105; riot in
    Jeddah, 133n15

Qahtan (tribe), 121, 123, 124
al-Qa'ida, 106
qal'ats, 31–37; Hisn Juhfah, 33–34,
    35, 42; Qal'at Abyar Naseef, 33;
    Qal'at Dukhan, 35–36; Qal'at
    Hafirah, 33, 34; Qal'at Khulays,
    35; Qal'at Shajwa, 33; Qal'at
    Usfan, 35, 36
Qarmatians, 115
Qassim, 76
qibla, 26
Qiblatayn mosque, 26
Quba'a Mosque, 25–26, 59
Qur'an, 125–27, 132n4; authority,
    91, 125–27; concerning adultery,
    25; concerning angels, 97; con-
    cerning Christianity, 88; concern-
    ing House of David, 94;
    concerning Jews, 19; concerning
    jinn, 91–92, 94, 95; concerning
    Kaaba, 134n4; concerning magic,
    79; concerning moon goddesses,
    97; concerning Najran, 114; con-
    cerning other religions, 84, 86, 88,
    98;   interpretation of, 126–27;
    translations, 91, 125–27; verses,
    during hajj, 55; verses, embroi-
    dered on the kiswa, 29–30; verses,
    used in magic, 76, 78, 79. See also
    Muhammad
Quraysh (tribe), 11, 24–25, 27,
    96–98

Qurayyah, 107, 109, 134n2

Rawwafah, 112, 112
Reginald, Prince of Chatillon, 32
religious freedom, 74–75, 84–89, 91,
    95. See also Wahhabis: discrimina-
    tion/intolerance
revolts. See protests/uprisings
rites. See eid rites; hajj rites

Saladin, 32, 115
Sanaa, 97
Saperstein, Rabbi David, 84, 86
sayy, 52, 55–56, 57, 65
Shahran (tribe), 123
Sharia, 79, 80–83, 85; concerning
    magic, 76–77. See also legal system
Shia, 12, 68, 88, 99, 115; discrimina-
    tion against, 22–23, 88, 100, 115
spice trade, 2, 10, 31, 115. See also
    trade routes
status: economic/social, xiv, 3, 11,
    18, 74; of women, 1–2, 3, 95,
    96–97
Sufis, 12, 92, 126, 133n16
sunna, 99, 126
Sunnis, 12, 68, 88, 99, 100

Tabuk, 106, 107–13
Tabuk Agricuiltural Development
    Corporation (TADCO), 108
Taliban, 95, 132n11
taqiyya, 115
tawwaf, 52, 54, 57, 58, 64–65, 69,
    132–33n13
terrorism, xvi; al-Kohbar Towers,
    100; OPM/SANG bombing, 100;
    September 11th, xiii, xv, xvii, 95
terrorists, xv, xvi, xvii, 95, 106; as
    jinn, 95; during hajj, 50
Tihama, 121, 123

tourism, 17, 19, 103–4, 130n1; developing, 106, 116, 118, 119; during hajj, 49–50, 58–61. *See also* pilgrimage trade

trade routes, 10–11, 31, 96–97, 114, 115, 118, 125; raids on, 10, 103. *See also* Darb Zubaydah; King's Highway

tribes, 103; in the Asir, 123–24; marriage between, 124; taxes, 124. *See also under names of specific tribes*

Tuba'a al-Himyari, King, 27

ibn Ubayy, Abdallah, 131n6

al-Ukhdud, 114

umra, 20, 47, 54. *See also* hajj

U.S. Commission on International Religious Freedom (USCIRF), 84

Wadi Qaraqir, 113

Wahhabis, 132n4, 132n11; conservatism, 87, 126–27; control by, xiv, 14, 15, 100 (see also *mutawwa'in*); discrimination/intolerance, 22–23, 88, 95–96, 99–101, 115 (*see also* religious freedom); and education, 14, 15, 73, 100, 104; extremists, 95, 127, 133n14; future of, 100–101

Wahhabism, 95–96, 99–100, 132n4, 132n11; and Al Saud, xiv, xvi, xvii, 14, 100–101; and Qur'an, 96, 126–27, 132n4

ibn Waleed, Khalid, 98

women: and hajj, 52, 53, 57, 58, 131n1; and *jinn*, 77; and magic, 77; and marriage, 3–7; treatment of, 1–2, 3, 14, 95, 96–97, 100

World Assembly of Muslim Youth (WAMY), 4–7

Zam-Zam spring, 20, 55, 65

Zubaydah, 37

About the Author

MARK A. CAUDILL is a 15-year U.S. Foreign Service officer who served in Jeddah, Saudi Arabia, from 1999 to 2002. Currently he is Vice Consul, U.S. Consulate General, Istanbul, Turkey.